T0386295

NARUTO

The Unofficial
COOKBOOK

NARUTO

The Unofficial
COOKBOOK

TITAN
BOOKS

LONDON

Contents

INTRODUCTION

Given that Naruto is also the name of a popular ramen topping, it's no surprise that food has a special presence in the *Naruto* anime and manga. From iconic moments, like experiencing the Curry of Life, to everyday scenes of villagers enjoying dumplings at a small street stall, food itself often is an important character in the series! As fans, it's only natural that we celebrate the wide array of food seen on the show. And, of course, finally get our chance to eat it!

The dishes gathered in this book are an assortment of food seen in, and inspired by, the world of Naruto. Ichiraku Ramen, the noodle shop where Naruto is practically a full-time resident, is a prominent example. But character favorites, like Chōji's Chips, and inspired dishes like Kurama's Nine-Tails Kitsune Udon, will immerse you—and your appetite—even further in the shinobi world.

The food depicted in *Naruto* is heavily influenced by Japanese cuisine, so this book also serves as a good introduction to Japanese-style cooking. To help you advance from a cooking Genin to a kitchen Hokage, each chapter begins with a ninja mission that will teach you an essential skill or technique. As in the missions doled out by high-ranking shinobi, each of these assignments is ranked from D (beginner) to B (advanced). (Sorry, Genin, no A- or S-ranked missions for you!) Once you complete them, your knowledge of Japanese cuisine will be solid enough to see you through any future culinary challenges that come your way!

THE COOK-NIN'S PANTRY

Like every cuisine, Japanese cooking has its own special ingredients that make it what it is. Some, like soy sauce, you're likely already familiar with, but others, like kombu, may be new to you. Most of the ingredients needed in this book can be found in your local grocery store, which is a good place to start your search–you may be surprised to see what's available in that "international" aisle that you usually skip past. But for others, you might need to visit an Asian grocery store or search online. (Which is much easier than traveling to the Forest of Death!) Many of these can be bought bottled, canned, or dried, so buy in bulk and stock up.

ABURAAGE
Availability: Challenging
A type of tofu product, aburaage is made by deep-frying thinly sliced tofu. It is usually prepared by cutting it into strips, or along the side and then opened like a pocket, similar to pita bread. It's often served seasoned, and preseasoned aburaage can be found in cans, but plain aburaage is typically sold frozen.

BAMBOO SHOOTS
Availability: Moderate
These are the young shoots of the bamboo plant. Fresh bamboo shoots are a symbol of spring and available for only a short time. Canned bamboo shoots are available all year.

BONITO FLAKES
Availability: Challenging
Labeled as *katsuobushi* in Japanese, these are shavings from dried bonito fish (a relative of mackerel and tuna). Bonito flakes are a staple in Japanese kitchens, used as the basis for making dashi, but also as a topping to sprinkle on pretty much anything.

DAIKON RADISH
Availability: Challenging
A large, round white root vegetable, daikon has a crunchy texture. It's a great addition to stir-fries and stews, excellent for pickling, and also popular to grate and use as a condiment alongside meat dishes.
Substitutions: If necessary, you can substitute regular radishes for texture, but the daikon's flavor is more peppery.

DASHI
Availability: Moderate
Made from bonito flakes and seaweed, this is the basic stock used in Japanese cooking. You'll learn how to make your own in the first chapter of this book! Otherwise, instant dashi granules are quite an excellent substitute, and sold in little bottles that you can keep on hand.
Substitutions: Chicken or vegetable broth

EDAMAME
Availability: Easy
These green young soybeans have become increasingly popular in the West. You'll find them sold both shelled and unshelled. They're typically found in the frozen food section of your supermarket.

FURIKAKE
Availability: Moderate
A dry or semidry condiment that's sprinkled on top of dishes, furikake typically contains sesame and seaweed, alongside a few other flavorings. It's easy to make yourself, as you'll see in the first recipes of this book!

GINGER
Availability: Easy
You're probably familiar with this pungent kitchen spice in some form already, but we're not talking about the powdered ginger in the spice cabinet! Fresh ginger root is used extensively in Japanese cuisine. Keep fresh ginger wrapped in plastic wrap in the fridge or freezer between uses.

HARUSAME
Availability: Moderate
Translated as "spring rain," *harusame* is the Japanese word for Chinese cellophane or glass noodles. Sold dried, they are very thin and translucent when cooked.

JAPANESE RICE
Availability: Easy
The most common type of rice in Japan is medium-grain rice, sometimes labeled as sushi rice. It has a unique, sticky texture that other types of rice cannot replicate. Getting your hands on good Japanese rice is essential for sushi and onigiri.

KOMBU
Availability: Challenging
This thick, dark, leathery dried seaweed is used mainly for making dashi. A little goes a long way in terms of flavor.

MIRIN

Availability: Moderate

A sweet, fortified rice-based liquor, mirin is used for cooking, never drinking. Mirin is one of the core flavors in Japanese cooking, and it's essential in recipes for the most authentic taste. Hon-mirin is naturally made mirin with about 20 percent alcohol content, whereas aji-mirin is an almost alcohol-free mirin substitute.

Substitutions: Sweet sherry, marsala wine, white grape juice

MISO

Availability: Moderate

A salty fermented soybean paste, miso is often made with wheat, rice, or barley mixed in. It's highly nutritious, and delicious. The most versatile type is white miso (actually a light brown color). Miso keeps practically forever in the fridge, so don't be afraid to buy a larger container.

MOCHI

Availability: Challenging

These Japanese rice cakes can be found in many varieties, some sweetened, some stuffed, some flavored, some plain. When including them in recipes, you'll want to use a plain variety, typically sold dried and individually sealed. If you're lucky, though, you'll find fresher mochi in the refrigerated or freezer section of Asian groceries.

MOCHIKO RICE FLOUR

Availability: Challenging

Sometimes labeled as glutinous rice flour, this flour is derived from sweet rice, a small-grain rice with a high starch content. It is much stickier than regular rice flour, and it's what gives mochi and other rice cakes their dense, chewy texture.

NORI

Availability: Moderate

A dried seaweed processed into paperlike sheets for sushi, this is the most common seaweed variety available outside Japan. Store it in airtight packaging in the pantry between uses to keep the sheets crisp. If it turns stale, hold a sheet a few inches over an open flame for a few seconds until the color turns a little darker to revive the flavor.

RICE VINEGAR

Availability: Easy

A mild vinegar suitable for salad dressings and marinades, rice vinegar is sold both plain and seasoned, ready for making sushi.

Substitutions: White wine vinegar

SAKE

Availability: Easy

The favorite alcohol of Japan, sake is a beverage made from fermented rice. Sake is a key flavor in Japanese cuisine, used to downplay the gamy flavor of fish and meat.

Substitutions: Dry sherry, Chinese rice wine, white wine

SESAME OIL

Availability: Easy

Made from sesame seeds, sesame oil has a rich, deep flavor. The different types of sesame oil reflect how toasted the sesame is, but go with a regular or light sesame oil for most dishes.

SESAME SEEDS

Availability: Easy

Both black and white sesame seeds are used in Japanese cooking, typically toasted and lightly crushed to bring out more of the nutty flavor trapped inside.

SHICHIMI TOGARASHI

Availability: Moderate

A spicy seasoning blend of seven spices (*shichi* meaning "seven", and *mi* meaning "flavor"), it's often used to add a little heat to noodles and soups.

SHIITAKE MUSHROOMS

Availability: Moderate

These mushrooms are available fresh or dried; dried shiitake work perfectly in recipes and are easy to reconstitute with water. Shiitake have a denser texture than other supermarket mushrooms like portabella, and the stems can be quite woody. So it's best to remove the stems from bigger shiitake mushrooms before cooking with them.

SHOCHU

Availability: Moderate

Shochu is a traditional Japanese hard liquor typically distilled from sweet potato, barley, or rice.

Substitutions: Vodka

SOBA NOODLES

Availability: Moderate

These thin noodles are made from buckwheat and have a subtle nutty flavor. Dried and frozen versions are available. You'll learn to make your own later in this book!

SOY SAUCE

Availability: Easy

A foundation ingredient of Japanese food, soy sauce comes in several varieties. Dark soy sauce is the most versatile, but light soy sauce has a sweeter, saltier flavor. Tamari is a thicker version best suited as a dipping sauce. Try to find a Japanese brand when shopping, because the flavors can differ between Asian cuisines.

SWEET RICE
Availability: Challenging
A very short-grain rice, this is sometimes labeled glutinous rice or mochigome. It has a super-sticky texture and is the basis for many rice cakes.

TOFU
Availability: Easy
There are two main types of this soybean product that are used in Japanese food: silken and firm. Firm tofu is more versatile, and can be used in countless dishes, whereas silken tofu is best enjoyed as is or in miso soup.

UDON NOODLES
Availability: Moderate
Thick and chewy, these noodles can be bought frozen or dried, but they're easy to make by hand! Frozen udon has a denser texture than dried noodles and can sometimes be found in the frozen food section of your market. You'll also learn to make your own later in this book!

UMEBOSHI
Availability: Challenging
A Japanese favorite that's believed to be good for digestion, these salty preserved plums are a popular addition to rice balls and sushi. They're pickled with the pits still intact, and the pulp is removed before adding them to dishes. Typically located in the refrigerated section, these are most likely found in grocery stores with a large Japanese or Asian food section.

WAKAME
Availability: Moderate
A dark green seaweed that's used in salads, soups, and vinegared dishes, this is the classic seaweed in miso soup. Sold dried, a little goes a long way; when reconstituting it, it will grow quite a few times in size.

YUZU KOSHO
Availability: Moderate
A versatile condiment made from chile, salt, and yuzu, its green varieties are typically spicier than the red ones. It's a popular addition to soups, sauces, and even sushi, and it is a great addition in marinades.

HOW TO BE A SUPERIOR COOK-NIN

Like the path to becoming a shinobi, mastering the culinary arts can seem intimidating. But follow this code of conduct, and you'll surely be Hokage of your kitchen one day.

A shinobi must prepare before it is too late.
Make sure you have all the ingredients and tools ready before you start cooking. Just like the concept of mise en place for a French kitchen, having everything portioned out and within reach at the very beginning of your cooking session ensures a smoother experience. There's nothing worse than being in the middle of a recipe and realizing that an important pan is soaking in the sink or the bag of rice you were going to use is almost empty.

A shinobi must follow their commander's instructions.
Read each recipe thoroughly, and understand the steps, before you begin. When you're deep into a mission, that's not a good time to realize you don't understand what to do next!

A shinobi knows their rank.
Just as the Hokage wouldn't send a barely trained Genin on an S-rank mission, if you're a beginning cook, it's wise not to start with the most difficult recipes. That's why the recipes in this book are ranked in difficulty from Genin (beginner) to Chūnin (intermediate) to Jōnin (advanced). That said, if (like Naruto) you want to test your ninjutsu with a harder challenge than you're used to, go for it! Just be patient if the result isn't what you hoped for.

A shinobi never gives up.
Learning new jutsus takes time! An apprentice sushi chef might wait years before they are allowed to prepare the rice. If a dish doesn't come out perfect the first time, don't let that deter you! A true shinobi knows there's a lesson in every failure. What went wrong, what could have been done better? Identifying your weaknesses helps you become an even more powerful kitchen ninja!

CHAPTER ONE: SOUPS AND APPETIZERS

A shinobi's life is fast-paced and exciting, to say the least! With the possibility of being sent on a sudden mission to a far-off place like the Land of Snow at any moment, sometimes you just have to make do with quick bites on the go. These recipes are perfect for snacking before, or during, an adventure. They're also great starters for a full meal with your team.

KONOHAGAKURE ACADEMY
MISSION #1: LET'S MAKE DASHI!

D-RANK

Every ninja of the Hidden Leaf Village begins as an academy student. To help you advance from galley Genin to kitchen Jōnin and beyond, each chapter of this book begins with a cook-nin assignment straight from Konohagakure Academy. Successfully complete these missions, and you will learn the basics of Japanese cooking . . . and be prepared to feed an entire team of hungry shinobi.

This first mission will teach you the basics of Japanese flavor. Dashi, a fish broth, is at the root of Japanese cuisine. Ever had miso soup? You've had dashi! Not just used for soups, dashi is the basis for many recipes, adding subtle umami to a dish's flavor profile. You can use instant dashi granules in a pinch, but being able to make dashi from scratch is an essential skill for an aspiring cook-nin. (And don't mention instant dashi if you happen to be in Ichiraku . . . Teuchi will likely toss you out!)

CLASSIC DASHI

LEVEL: GENIN
PREP TIME: 5 MINUTES
COOK TIME: 25 MINUTES
YIELD: 6 SERVINGS
SPECIAL EQUIPMENT: FINE-MESH SIEVE

8 cups water

One 5-inch strip dried kombu

¼ ounce bonito flakes, about 1 cup

Place the water in a large saucepan and add the kombu.

Let the kombu soak for about 30 minutes, then bring to a boil over medium heat. Let simmer for about 5 minutes, then pull out the kombu and discard.

Turn the heat down to low, add the bonito flakes, and stir to submerge them.

Let simmer for about 5 minutes, skimming off any foam, then turn off the heat and let steep for 15 minutes.

Strain the dashi through a fine-mesh sieve into a medium bowl. Discard the bonito flakes, or set aside to make furikake.

Dashi can be stored in a sealed container in the fridge for up to 3 days before use.

SUBSTITUTION JUTSU: VEGETARIAN DASHI

To make vegetarian dashi, fill a sealable container with the water and kombu, and add ¼ cup of dried shiitake mushrooms. Let sit in the refrigerator for at least 24 hours. Filter the resulting broth through a fine-mesh sieve into a medium bowl. Discard the kombu and mushrooms, or set aside to make furikake.

LEFTOVER DASHI FURIKAKE

LEVEL: GENIN
PREP TIME: 5 MINUTES
COOK TIME: 10 MINUTES
YIELD: 6 SERVINGS

1 cup used bonito flakes from dashi (see previous recipe)

1 tablespoon sesame oil

1 teaspoon sesame seeds

2 tablespoons soy sauce

2 tablespoons mirin

1 teaspoon sugar

Add the bonito flakes and sesame oil to a wide skillet over medium heat. Stir for a few minutes until most of the moisture has been cooked off, then add the sesame seeds and let cook until fragrant.

Turn the heat to low and add the soy sauce, mirin, and sugar to the pan. Cook until all excess moisture is evaporated, stirring thoroughly to break up any clumps in the flakes.

Anything goes when it comes to furikake; sprinkle it on top of rice or noodle dishes, mix it into your favorite onigiri, or even sprinkle some on top of soups!

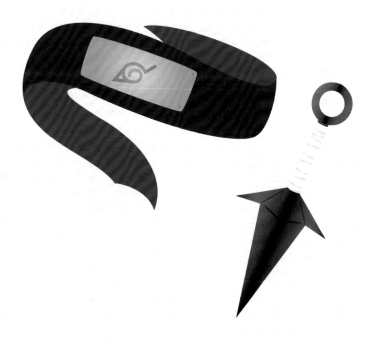

KAKASHI'S EGGPLANT-MIXED MISO SOUP

This recipe is said to be a favorite of Kakashi Hatake. Perhaps that's because, like him, eggplant is a humble ingredient, yet versatile enough to be effective in a variety of situations. Eggplant also tends to wonderfully absorb whatever flavors it's cooked in, much like the famed copy ninja who's picked up myriad ninja techniques. In Japan, miso soup isn't just one recipe—it changes with the seasons and what is available on hand. This is a good base recipe, but feel free to add whatever ingredients you like! A ninja must be able to improvise, after all.

LEVEL: GENIN
PREP TIME: 5 MINUTES
COOK TIME: 20 MINUTES
YIELD: 4 SERVINGS

4 cups dashi (use instant dashi or make your own; see recipe, page 15)

1 small Japanese eggplant, or ½ American eggplant, cubed

2 sheets aburaage, cut into strips

3 tablespoons miso

1 bunch green onions, finely chopped

Add the dashi to a small pot over medium heat and bring to a boil. Add the eggplant and aburaage and let simmer for about 10 minutes, until the eggplant is softened.

Turn the heat down to low, then ladle a small scoop of the broth into a small bowl. Add the miso to the bowl, then stir well with a spoon until the miso is completely dissolved, using the spoon to mash the miso against the sides of the bowl as you go.

Pour the broth mix back into the pot and stir to combine, taking care not to let the pot reach a boil again. You don't want your miso to get grainy!

Just before serving, add the green onions to the pot and let simmer for about 1 minute, then portion into bowls to serve.

KONOHA MIXED MUSHROOM SOUP

Healthy, flavorful, and simple, mushrooms are a truly wonderful recipe ingredient (except for the chakra-absorbing kind that Naruto and Might Guy ate while traveling on the Sea of Silence—stay away from those). This recipe is rumored to hark back to the early days of the Hidden Leaf Village, and may even have been created by its founder and First Hokage, Hashirama Senju. By village tradition, the soup is prepared using whatever mushrooms are on hand, an invaluable option for shinobi chefs on the go.

LEVEL: GENIN
PREP TIME: 5 MINUTES
COOK TIME: 35 MINUTES
YIELD: 4 SERVINGS

3 tablespoons sesame oil, divided

2 cups roughly chopped assorted Japanese mushrooms (shiitake, enoki, etc.)

1 white onion, roughly chopped

3 cloves garlic, minced

¼ cup sake

¼ cup mirin

3 cups dashi

1 tablespoon soy sauce

1 bunch green onions, finely chopped

Japanese pepper

Place a wide pot over medium heat and, once hot, add half the oil. Add the mushrooms and cook for about 5 minutes, until the edges start to brown and the mushrooms turn soft. Transfer the mushrooms to a small bowl and set aside.

Add the remaining oil to the pan along with the white onion. Turn the heat down to medium low and let the onion cook for 15 to 20 minutes, until it has started to caramelize.

Add the garlic and cook a few minutes more, then add the mushrooms, sake, mirin, dashi, and soy sauce. Cover with a tight-fitting lid, turn the heat to low, and simmer for about 10 minutes.

A few minutes before serving, add the green onions and let simmer for a few minutes until they've softened. Add pepper to taste and serve.

NINJA-DOG NIKUMAN

The Inazuka clan is known for its close relationship with its dogs, signified by the red fang-like markings on clan members' cheeks. This recipe honors the clan with meaty steamed buns adorned with Inazuka symbols, a satisfying snack for any carnivore. The contents are easily customized for your particular meat tooth; maybe you'd like to use some barbecued meat, or add a little spice for extra heat? Serve alone or with soy sauce on the side.

LEVEL: CHŪNIN
PREP TIME: 2 HOURS
COOK TIME: 12 MINUTES PER BATCH
YIELD: 12 BUNS
SPECIAL EQUIPMENT: BAMBOO STEAMER

FOR THE FILLING

3 dried shiitake mushrooms

½ cup shredded cabbage

1 tablespoon salt

¾ pound ground pork

2 green onions, thinly sliced

1 inch fresh ginger, grated

3 cloves garlic, minced

¼ teaspoon cornstarch

1 tablespoon soy sauce

1 tablespoon sake

1 teaspoon sesame oil

1 teaspoon sugar

FOR THE DOUGH

1 teaspoon instant yeast

2 teaspoons sugar

1¾ cups all-purpose flour

1 teaspoon baking powder

¼ teaspoon kosher salt

2 tablespoons neutral oil

1 cup dashi

Red food coloring

Start on the filling by prepping some of the ingredients. First rehydrate the mushrooms by placing them in a small bowl of warm water to soak until softened, about 10 minutes. While they're soaking, place the cabbage in a medium bowl and sprinkle with the salt. Mix together, then set aside.

Work on the dough. Combine the yeast, sugar, flour, baking powder, salt, and oil in a large bowl. Add the dashi and mix until a ball starts to form. If it feels dry, add a little bit of water until the dough comes together.

Turn the dough out onto a lightly floured surface and knead for about 10 minutes, until it becomes smooth and elastic. Form into a round and place the dough into a lightly oiled bowl. Cover loosely with a kitchen towel and allow it to rise in a warm spot for roughly an hour, until doubled in size.

While the dough is rising, come back to the filling. Remove as much excess water as you can from the cabbage by taking a handful at a time and squeezing gently, then placing it into a large bowl. Squeeze excess moisture out of the mushrooms as well, then chop finely. Add the mushrooms to the cabbage, then add all the remaining filling ingredients. Mix to combine. Cover the bowl and set in the fridge until ready to use.

Prepare the basket linings by taking sheets of parchment paper and cutting out twelve 3-by-3-inch squares.

Turn the dough out onto a lightly floured surface and divide into 13 equal portions. Set one aside to use for the decorative markings. Take the remaining portions and shape into balls, then use a rolling pin to flatten them into rounds. The edges should be a little thinner than the middle to make it easier to pinch them closed. Working with one round at a time, place a spoonful of the filling in the center of the dough. Bring the edges together on top of the filling at four points, then twist and press down to

continues on page 22

seal completely. Sit each bun seam-side down on a parchment paper square and let rest.

Create the clan markings by adding a drop of food coloring at a time to the remaining dough, then kneading it in until evenly it's distributed and a bright red color is achieved. Use a rolling pin to flatten the dough into a rectangle, then use a knife to cut out twelve pairs of triangles, each about ½-inch long.

Use a pastry brush to brush water on the surface of each bun, then arrange one triangle on top of each bun with the base of the triangle at the top and the tips of the triangles pointed downward. Press down lightly to adhere them to the buns. Set the buns aside to let rest for another 15 minutes.

Bring a large pot of water to a boil. Arrange the buns in the trays of a bamboo steamer, making sure to leave a little space between them as they might expand more while cooking. Depending on the size of your steamer, you may be able to cook them in one batch. If not, place only as many as will fit comfortably and repeat for subsequent batches. Place the bamboo steamer on top of the pot and steam over high heat for 12 minutes.

Serve warm.

TSUNADE'S HEALING ZOSUI

Considered the world's greatest medical-nin, master healer Tsunade knows that the best way to heal is to nourish body and soul. This zosui, or classic rice soup, is like a Japanese version of chicken noodle soup. It's great to whip up anytime you're feeling under the weather (and Tsunade isn't available).

LEVEL: GENIN
PREP TIME: 15 MINUTES
COOK TIME: 20 MINUTES
YIELD: 4 SERVINGS

4–6 sliced and simmered radishes for garnish

3½ cups dashi, divided

2 boneless, skinless chicken thighs, chopped

1 carrot, sliced

3 shiitake mushrooms, chopped

1½ cups cooked Japanese rice

1 tablespoon soy sauce

1 large egg

3 green onions, chopped

1 teaspoon toasted sesame seeds

¼ teaspoon pepper

Cut the radishes into ¼-inch slices, then trim them down into a diamond shape.

Place ½ cup of dashi in a small pot over high heat and bring to a boil. When boiling, add the radishes, then turn off the heat and let cool. If preparing in advance, transfer the radishes and liquid to a sealed container, then store in the fridge until ready to use. Otherwise, transfer the radishes to a small bowl and discard the broth.

When ready to prepare the soup, place 3 cups of dashi in a wide pot over medium heat and bring to a boil.

Add the chicken and carrot to the boiling dashi, then cover and turn the heat down to medium low. Cook for 5 minutes, then add the mushrooms, rice, and soy sauce. Cover and continue cooking for about 10 minutes.

Whisk the egg in a small bowl, then slowly drizzle the beaten egg into the pot. Add the green onion, sesame seeds, and pepper on top, then cover and let cook for a few minutes, just enough for the egg to set.

When ready to serve, portion out into individual bowls and top each with a simmered radish diamond.

SUBSTITUTION JUTSU

To make a vegetarian version, use vegetarian dashi and leave out the chicken. Cubes of firm tofu can be added, if desired, to balance out the flavor of the mushrooms.

CHŌJI'S CHIPS

Chōji Akimichi always seems to be snacking, but that's for a good reason: When your signature jutsus involve converting calories to chakra, you need extra calories on hand. What's better for this than portable, snackable, calorie-packed chips? Japanese food makers have created many unusual chip flavors, like cod roe (give it a try sometime). But for the practical shinobi, these classic flavors are easy and satisfying to make at home.

LEVEL: CHŪNIN
PREP TIME: 30 MINUTES
COOK TIME: 20 MINUTES
YIELD: 6 SERVINGS
SPECIAL EQUIPMENT: SPICE GRINDER OR FOOD PROCESSOR, MANDOLINE, KITCHEN THERMOMETER

FOR THE SEASONING

SEAWEED FLAVOR JUTSU

1 tablespoon sea salt

1 sheet nori

RAMEN FLAVOR JUTSU

1 packet of instant ramen powdered seasoning

SESAME FLAVOR JUTSU

1 tablespoon salt

1 tablespoon toasted sesame seeds

1 teaspoon garlic powder

FOR THE CHIPS

1 pound russet potatoes

1 quart ice water

Vegetable oil for frying

SUBSTITUTION JUTSU

Master the above varieties, then feel free to create new chip jutsus of your own. You can even take your favorite store-bought furikake and grind it up for your own spin on flavor!

Place ingredients for your desired seasoning mix into a spice grinder or food processor and blend until finely ground (not necessary if you're using ramen seasoning). Set aside.

Prepare the chips by using a mandoline or the wide edge of a box cutter to slice the potatoes to a thickness of ⅛ inch. Place them in a large bowl with enough of the ice water to cover them and let them soak for at least 30 minutes. Drain the potatoes using a colander or strainer, then pat dry thoroughly with paper towels.

Heat approximately 2 inches of oil in a wide pot to 375°F.

Use tongs or a slotted spoon to place a handful of slices in the oil at a time, taking care to not crowd the pan too much to prevent temperature from dropping. Fry for about 4 minutes, until a golden color is achieved, stirring frequently to ensure even cooking. You know they're close when the potatoes start bubbling less.

Remove the potatoes from the oil with a slotted spoon and transfer to paper towels to dry. If necessary, add more oil and wait for the oil to come back up to temperature before frying another batch.

While the subsequent batches are frying, pat down the freshly fried chips to remove as much oil as possible, then immediately transfer them to a large bowl and sprinkle some of the seasoning on top.

Continue adding more chips to the top of the bowl after they're done frying and have been patted dry, then season them. Letting excess seasoning fall onto the chips below maximizes flavor!

Repeat until all slices have been cooked, dried, and seasoned.

The chips are best enjoyed fresh, but can be stored in an airtight container for up to 3 days.

SHURIKEN SENBEI

Rice crackers known as senbei are super-popular snacks in Japan, and—as with the favored ninja weapon—different regions are known for their own styles. In this recipe, frying the dough limits how neatly the crackers can be shaped; no shinobi would mistake them for actual throwing stars. But it boosts the flavor tremendously!

LEVEL: CHŪNIN
PREP TIME: 15 MINUTES
COOK TIME: 20 MINUTES
YIELD: 12 SERVINGS
SPECIAL EQUIPMENT: FOOD PROCESSOR, KITCHEN THERMOMETER

½ cup mochiko rice flour

1 cup cooked Japanese rice

¼ teaspoon salt

¼ teaspoon baking powder

1 tablespoon sesame oil

¼ cup water

2 tablespoons sesame seeds

Vegetable oil for frying

To make the dough, place the rice flour, rice, salt, baking powder and oil in a food processor. Run until finely ground. Add the water, then pulse the processor until the water is fully incorporated. It will still be dry, but the dough should clump together when pressed. If not, add a tablespoon of water at a time until the right consistency is achieved.

Scoop out the dough into a small bowl, then add sesame seeds and work them into the dough until they're evenly distributed.

Roll the dough out on a sheet of parchment paper to a thickness of about ¼ inch or thinner, then cut into shuriken shapes. A four-pointed star, besides being a favorite of a shinobi, is more likely to hold together than more complex shapes. For bonus points, cut out a hole in the middle using a straw or knife.

To fry the senbei, heat about 2 inches of oil to 375°F in a small, deep pot. Once it's hot, gently place a few crackers at a time in the oil, taking care not to overcrowd the pan. Fry for about 3 to 5 minutes, flipping occasionally to ensure even browning. Once a golden color is achieved, remove from the oil with a slotted spoon and place on paper towels to absorb excess oil.

SUBSTITUTION JUTSU

Counting your calories? These crackers can also be baked! Arrange the shuriken on parchment-lined baking sheets and spray the tops with a neutral oil. Bake at 350°F for 12 to 15 minutes, watching them closely and removing once the dough starts to turn golden. They will be soft at first but firm up as they cool. The flavor is different from the fried version but still tasty.

CHAPTER TWO: RICE DISHES

You may think you've tasted rice. But like the fighting prowess of the Great Toad Sage, rice preparation in Japanese cuisine is in a league of its own. From flavorful curries to fresh sushi, or even just sprinkled with a dash of salt, this versatile carb is the essential energy behind any ninja's most powerful jutsus!

KONOHAGAKURE ACADEMY
MISSION #2: LET'S MASTER PERFECT RICE!

Having mastered flavor by learning to make dashi, you're now ready for your next assignment. Rice is by far *the* staple food of Japan, which has been cultivating it for more than two thousand years. At one point it was even used as currency! Given the fact that the word for cooked rice, *gohan*, has become synonymous with the term "meal," it's clear that mastering rice is a must for any cook-nin! But not to worry; like a complex jutsu that's taught one hand seal at a time, basic rice preparation is a breeze if you follow some simple steps!

Japanese rice has a higher starch content than long-grain rice varieties such as basmati. So even if you have a rice cooker, the extra starch should always be removed before cooking. Perfectly made rice has plump yet firm individual grains that cling to one another; excess starch turns them into a big lump of mush.

Rice-polishing jutsu, water-style cloud cleansing technique:
To remove surplus starch from your rice, place the rice in a large bowl and add enough water to cover it. "Polish" the rice by gently scrubbing it between your hands, noticing the cloudiness of the water as you do. When the water stops getting cloudier, carefully pour out the liquid and then rinse the rice under a faucet, stirring and repeating a few times until the water runs clear. Drain thoroughly using a fine-mesh sieve or colander.

JAPANESE STEAMED RICE

LEVEL: GENIN
PREP TIME: 10 MINUTES
COOK TIME: 25 MINUTES
YIELD: 6 SERVINGS
SPECIAL EQUIPMENT: FINE-MESH SIEVE

2 cups Japanese medium-grain white rice

2½ cups water

1 teaspoon salt

Polish the rice to remove excess starch, then drain well with a fine-mesh sieve or colander.

Place the rice, water, and salt into a heavy-bottomed pot. Turn the heat to high and bring the water just to boiling, then immediately turn the heat down to low and put on a tight-fitting lid.

Leave the rice to steam for about 15 minutes, until you see small, even dimples across the surface of the rice, and all the water has been absorbed.

Turn the heat to high for 1 more minute to allow any last bit of water to evaporate, then remove from the heat. Crack the lid open, and leave to rest for 10 minutes.

Remove the lid and gently fluff the rice with a rice paddle or wooden spoon before serving.

SUBSTITUTION JUTSU: SUSHI RICE

2 cups Japanese-style medium-grain white rice
2 cups water
1 teaspoon instant dashi granules
½ cup sushi vinegar

To make sushi-style rice, cook the rice in the same way as basic steamed rice, setting aside the sushi vinegar. Once the rice is cooked, transfer the hot rice to a wide, shallow bowl and pour in the rice vinegar. Gently fold the rice with a rice paddle or wooden spoon for a few minutes, until the rice looks glossy and is no longer steaming. Sushi rice should be enjoyed at room temperature, not refrigerated.

SASUKE'S FAVORITE ONIGIRI

Whether you're a ninja on a mission or an office worker on a break, this portable, easily customized rice snack is a delicious and sensible choice. Ever practical and mission-focused, Sasuke favors two classic flavorings: okaka, which is bonito flakes with soy sauce, and freshly prepared tomatoes. Other popular fillings include pickled plums, mayo with canned tuna, or various flavors of furikake.

LEVEL: CHŪNIN
PREP TIME: 15 MINUTES
YIELD: 8 SERVINGS

¼ cup bonito flakes

2 teaspoons soy sauce

1 fresh tomato, or 1 of Sasuke's Soy-Pickled Tomatoes (page 97)

2 sheets nori

4 cups freshly cooked Japanese short-grain rice

2 tablespoons sesame seeds, toasted

Begin to prepare the filling by mixing the bonito flakes with the soy sauce.

Quarter the tomato, remove as much of the pulp as you can, then chop into small pieces.

Toast the nori sheets briefly, holding them a few inches over an open flame such as a lighter or a gas stove burner on low, until the color darkens. Then cut into eight squares.

To shape the onigiri, place a small bowl of salted water to the side to use for rinsing your hands. Keeping your hands wet, flatten out ½ cup of rice in your hands and make an indentation in the middle, placing a small amount of either the okaka or tomatoes in the center.

Gently round the rice over the top of the filling, then press together firmly with your hands. Shape it into a ball, or, if you're feeling extra fancy, a flattened triangle.

To finish, sprinkle some sesame seeds on top of each onigiri, then place it in a nori square and press the nori firmly into the rice to adhere it to the surface. Set aside and continue with the remaining rice, rewetting your hands as needed.

Serve at room temperature for best texture.

continues on page 34

SUBSTITUTION JUTSU: DEIDARA'S BAKUDAN ONIGIRI

For Deidara, explosives are a true art form. Fortunately, with these bomb-shaped rice balls—which also resemble shinobi smoke bombs—the only explosion is an explosion of flavor. KATSU!

4 cups freshly cooked rice
4 tablespoons onigiri filling (bonito flakes, leftover dashi furikake, etc.)
4 sheets nori, cut into strips

Follow the recipe for Sasuke's Favorite Onigiri (page 33). After adding the filling, smooth out the surface by rolling the rice gently between both hands, creating a ball.

To finish, take a sheet of nori and carefully wrap it around the rice ball, adding a drop of water on the nori as needed to make it more pliable and help it stick to the surface of the rice. Keep adding strips to the ball to cover the remaining exposed rice, stopping when the rice is fully covered, resulting in a nori-wrapped ball. Three to four strips usually do the trick!

SAND VILLAGE SEKIHAN

Leave it to the Land of Wind to find a way to build a thriving city in the unforgiving desert. With beautiful dark beans scattered over rice, this dish somewhat resembles the Sand Village landscape. It can be made using only mochiko rice (a specific rice variety), but this recipe blends that with regular Japanese rice for a more balanced texture.

LEVEL: GENIN
PREP TIME: 4 HOURS
COOK TIME: 1 HOUR 30 MINUTES
YIELD: 2 SERVINGS
SPECIAL EQUIPMENT: METAL COOKING CHOPSTICKS

⅓ cup dried adzuki beans, soaked in water overnight

4 cups water

1 cup mochiko rice

1 cup Japanese rice

1 teaspoon salt

1 tablespoon black sesame seeds

Place the beans and 2 cups of water in a small pot over high heat. Bring to a boil, then cook for about 5 minutes. Strain the beans, discarding the water.

Return the beans to the pot and add the remaining 2 cups of water. Cover loosely and bring to a simmer over high heat. Reduce the heat to low and let simmer for about 30 minutes, until the beans are soft and break when pressed between your fingers.

Drain the beans, reserving the cooking liquid in a separate container. Set both the beans and liquid aside.

Polish the rice as described at the beginning of this chapter (page 30), then place in a small pot along with cooked beans, salt, and 2 cups of the reserved bean liquid. Cover with a tight-fitting lid, then turn the heat to high and bring just to boiling.

Immediately turn the heat down to low and leave the rice to steam for about 15 minutes, until you see small, even dimples across the surface of the rice and all the water has been absorbed.

Turn the heat to high for 1 more minute to allow any last bit of water to evaporate, then remove from the heat. Cover, leaving the lid cracked open, and leave to rest for 10 minutes.

To serve, gently fluff the rice with a spatula or rice paddle, then garnish with the sesame seeds arranged in the shape of the Sand Village logo.

SHADOW CLONE JUTSU: HINATA'S NARUTO ONIGIRI

While the series Naruto *mainly focuses on ninja, there are special moments when food takes the stage. By mastering our secret shadow clone jutsus, you can bring a select few of those iconic dishes into the real world!*

Having a crush on someone who doesn't have a clue, soft-spoken Hinata is in a tough spot! Try as she might, Naruto seems oblivious to her efforts. Knowing that the surest way to a shinobi's heart is through his stomach (literally, during combat, as well as figuratively), she creates a Naruto-inspired onigiri just for him, to help get her message across.

LEVEL: CHŪNIN
PREP TIME: 5 MINUTES
COOK TIME: 20 MINUTES
YIELD: 2 SERVINGS

FOR THE TAMAGOYAKI (OR GRILLED EGG)

2 large eggs

1 teaspoon sugar

½ teaspoon salt

Neutral oil

FOR THE ONIGIRI

1 teaspoon salt

1 carrot

1 radish

1 sheet nori

2 cups freshly cooked rice

1 roll narutomaki, sliced to ¼-inch thickness (fish cake available from Asian grocery stores, or make your own; see page 64 for fish cakes)

1 teaspoon bonito flakes

To prepare the tamagoyaki, whisk the eggs, sugar, and salt in a small bowl until well combined.

Place a small skillet over medium-low heat, and once hot, spray or coat with oil, then pour the egg mixture into the pan. Cover with a tight-fitting lid, then let cook until the egg is set, about 5 minutes.

Remove the eggs from the pan and let cool, then cut into ten small triangles.

To prepare the onigiri, place a bowl of hot water to the side and add the salt and stir until dissolved. Using a potato peeler, scrape the carrot into thin strips, then place in the bowl.

Cut the radish into thin disks, then add to the bowl as well. Let sit for about 10 minutes to allow the vegetables to soften, then remove them from the bowl and gently squeeze to remove excess water.

To assemble, first prepare the nori. Following the score marks on the nori, cut two long strips about 1 inch wide to use for Naruto's headband. Use what's remaining of the sheet to cut strips about ⅛ inch wide for his whiskers and eyes.

Divide the rice into two portions, then gently press into a rounded triangular shape about 5 inches wide.

continues on page 38

Start assembling by arranging the egg triangles along the top for his hair, pressing them into the rice and shaping the rice up along the base of the egg if needed to get it to stay put.

Arrange two radish disks on the sides for his ears, pressing them into the rice in a similar manner.

Lay the wide nori strip along the top point of the triangle to create a headband, trimming it where it meets the egg to help it lay neatly. Place a slice of narutomaki in the center of the headband.

Using tweezers if needed, place some bonito flakes on either side for his cheeks, then lay the smaller nori strips in position to create Naruto's eyes and whiskers. To finish, use a carrot strip for his mouth.

MADARA-EYE INARIZUSHI

Onions have a strong flavor, but probably not strong enough to awaken the Rinnegan. Nevertheless, these tasty pickled onion-topped treats, which recall Madara Uchiha's distinctive eyes, might earn you the title God of Creation. Or God of Destruction, depending on your diners' love of onions. Some red onions have a purplish hue that's especially good for evoking Madara's evolved Sharingan.

LEVEL: GENIN
PREP TIME: 12 HOURS
COOK TIME: 20 MINUTES
YIELD: 8 SERVINGS

FOR THE PICKLED ONION

1 small red onion, quartered and thinly sliced

½ cup rice vinegar

½ cup water

2 tablespoons sugar

½ tablespoon salt

FOR THE INARIZUSHI

8 aburaage squares

3 tablespoons soy sauce

3 tablespoons sugar

1 cup dashi

2 cups water

3 cups sushi rice

1 tablespoon sesame seeds

Begin by preparing the pickled onions in advance. Place the onions in a small jar or container. Bring the vinegar, water, sugar, and salt just to a boil in a small pot over high heat, then stir until the sugar is melted. Pour the liquid over the onions, then cover and let sit in the fridge for at least 12 hours.

To prepare the inarizushi, bring a small pot of water to a boil over high heat. While it's warming up, prepare the aburaage by cutting along one side of each square to create a pouch. Use your hands or a knife to gently open up the pouch.

Boil the cut aburaage in hot water for a minute, then drain well.

Place the soy sauce, sugar, dashi, and water in a small pot and bring to a boil over high heat.

Once boiling, turn the heat down to medium, add the aburaage, and cook for 10 to 15 minutes. Transfer to an airtight container and place in the fridge until ready to use.

To assemble, mix the sushi rice and sesame seeds, then divide into eight portions.

Gently squeeze an aburaage pouch to remove excess liquid, then carefully stuff one of the rice portions into the pouch. Repeat for the remaining pouches.

Arrange strips of pickled onion in rows on top of the rice, with their arcs facing the center like parentheses. Trim the slices down as needed to match the width of the pouch. Tuck the edges of the onions into the pouch.

SHADOW CLONE JUTSU: SANSHŌ'S CURRY OF LIFE

If you've ever tasted Japanese curry, you can understand Rock Lee's obsession with Sanshō's Curry of Life. Packed with nourishment and flavor, and just the right amount of heat to light a fire in your spirit, it's a one-dish meal that can sustain body and soul! Each shinobi turns this dish into their own masterpiece, but here's a perfect base recipe to get you started on developing your own take on this potent dish.

LEVEL: GENIN
PREP TIME: 15 MINUTES
COOK TIME: 3 HOURS
YIELD: 8 SERVINGS

1 tablespoon vegetable oil or olive oil

1 pound stew beef, cubed

5 tablespoons butter, divided

4 large onions, roughly chopped

2 cloves garlic, minced

2 tablespoons garam masala

1 small apple, grated

Two 14.5-ounce cans diced tomatoes

One 6-ounce can tomato paste

5 cups beef stock

3 carrots, roughly chopped

4 potatoes, roughly chopped

2 tablespoons honey

1 tablespoon soy sauce

1 tablespoon Worcestershire sauce

2 tablespoons curry powder

2 tablespoons red chile powder

3 tablespoons all-purpose flour

1 cup frozen peas

2 tablespoons grated Parmesan

Place a large pot over medium heat. Add the oil, and when hot, add the beef. Cook until lightly browned on all sides, stirring only when the bottom of the beef touching the pan develops a nice brown color. Transfer the beef to a small bowl and set aside for later.

Add 3 tablespoons of the butter and the onions to the large pot and turn the heat down to low. Cover with a tight-fitting lid and cook for about 45 minutes, stirring occasionally, until the onions are a rich, brown color. Turn the heat up to medium and add the garlic. Cook for a few minutes, until fragrant.

While the garlic is cooking, place a small skillet over medium-low heat and add the garam masala. Toast for a few minutes, until fragrant and the color just starts to deepen, then add to the large pot. Add the apple, tomatoes, tomato paste, cooked beef, and beef stock, then cover and simmer on low for 1 hour.

Add the carrots, potatoes, honey, soy sauce, and Worcestershire sauce and simmer uncovered on low for 30 minutes.

To make a thickening roux, toast the curry powder and red chile powder in a small pot over medium heat until fragrant. Immediately add the remaining 2 tablespoons of butter, then turn down the heat to low and add the flour. Stir constantly until the mixture scrapes clean from the bottom of the pan. Scooping a ladleful at a time, incorporate the broth from the pot into the flour mixture, stirring thoroughly each time to blend the liquid into the flour before adding more. It will start off as a paste, but as more broth is added, it will start to thin out. Once the flour mixture has turned into a thin gravy, pour the gravy into the large pot. Cover again and cook on low for 30 minutes.

About 15 minutes before serving, add the peas and Parmesan and let the pot simmer uncovered until ready to serve.

UZUMAKI OMURICE

The Land of Whirlpools was once home to the Uzumaki clan, and though they've since scattered to different villages, they took their swirls with them! In fact, the Japanese word uzumaki *itself is derived from the words* uzu, *meaning swirl, and* maki, *or roll, so of course the symbolism of their namesake is never far behind them. As seen with the red swirl on the Konoha uniforms, the whirlpool motif turns up everywhere in the world of Naruto and is found throughout Japanese cuisine as well. Among the most iconic examples are the beautifully swirled omelets of master chefs. Getting that perfect swirl takes a bit of practice, as with the most difficult ninja arts. But in this case, that just means you'll have to eat more while perfecting it!*

LEVEL: JŌNIN
PREP TIME: 15 MINUTES
COOK TIME: 30 MINUTES
YIELD: 2 SERVINGS
SPECIAL EQUIPMENT: METAL COOKING CHOPSTICKS

FOR THE OMELET

4 large eggs

1 tablespoon heavy cream

½ teaspoon salt

1 tablespoon neutral oil

2 green onions, finely chopped (optional)

FOR THE RICE

1 tablespoon ketchup

1 tablespoon oyster sauce

1 tablespoon soy sauce

1 tablespoon mirin

2 slices bacon, cut into strips

3 cloves garlic, minced

1 carrot, diced

½ small onion, diced

2 tablespoons butter

2 cups cooked Japanese short-grain rice

Prepare the omelet by whisking together the eggs, heavy cream, and salt in a small bowl until combined. Let sit for at least 15 minutes so the salt can blend into the egg. This step is critical for good, fluffy eggs!

To start the rice, combine the ketchup, oyster sauce, soy sauce, and mirin and set aside.

Place a large skillet over medium heat. Add the bacon and cook until the edges start to brown, then add the garlic, carrot, and onion and cook until softened. Add the butter, and once it's melted, add the rice, breaking up the rice with a spatula.

Keep folding the rice over until it stops steaming, then stir in the prepared sauce and cook until most of the moisture has been absorbed by the rice. Remove from the heat.

To plate, spoon half of the rice into a small rice bowl, then place a plate upside down on top. Carefully invert the bowl, dumping the rice onto the plate in a perfect little mound. Repeat this process with the remaining rice for the other serving.

To make the omelet, heat a nonstick skillet over medium-low heat, and once it's hot, add the oil and place half of the egg mixture into the skillet.

Wait a few minutes for the egg to mostly coagulate and create a solid, cooked base, then grab your chopsticks! You want at least half of the egg mixture to be cooked at this point, otherwise the egg will tear.

Place the chopsticks on opposite sides of the pan, then slowly start to bring them together, stopping when they're about 2 inches apart, folding the egg up in between them as you do so. If your hands are agile enough and the chopsticks long enough, you may be able to do it one handed. Otherwise, hold one chopstick in each hand. If the egg starts to tear at all at this step, stop immediately and wait for the egg to cook a little more.

Once the chopsticks are gathered in the middle, twist! Hold the chopsticks firmly so they don't lose any distance from each other and retain the egg between them, then rotate the chopsticks in a circular motion, forming the gathered egg in the middle into a coil in the middle of the pan. By doing this, the remaining runny egg will start to spiral out onto the edges of the pan. Wait a few seconds to allow that egg to set, then it's ready to serve.

Use a spatula to gently slide the spiraled egg out of the pan and place on top of the rice mound.

Repeat this process with the other half of the egg mixture. Top with a swirl of ketchup and chopped green onion, if desired.

SUBSTITUTION JUTSU
Need a vegetarian option? Leave out the bacon, or swap it for finely chopped shiitake mushrooms.

CHAPTER THREE: NOODLE DISHES

Without ramen, Naruto wouldn't be who he is. Needing to care for himself at a young age, he found that economical and easy-to-prepare instant ramen was just the thing to make him self-sufficient, so of course he'd grow fond of it! After eating instant noodles for so long, imagine the bliss Naruto must have felt enjoying his first bowl of Ichiraku ramen! While it may be Naruto's favorite, ramen is only the tip of the iceberg when it comes to Japanese noodles. From toothsome udon to nutty soba, these nourishing carbs are a staple for keeping the fire in a ninja's spirit. And, in true Japanese style, don't forget to slurp!

KONOHAGAKURE ACADEMY MISSION #3: MAKE YOUR OWN HANDMADE NOODLES!

C-RANK

Dried noodles are convenient, but nothing beats a hot bowl of fresh ramen made from scratch. And as Naruto, Chōji, and Sakura learned while trying to make a perfect ramen recipe for Ayame's ransom, the true secret to a great bowl of noodles is that fresh-cut noodles just taste better! For this mission, you'll learn the noodle-making technique of Ichiraku Ramen owner Teuchi himself! (As told to us by Matsu and Nishi.)

Whether it be udon, ramen, or soba, the technique for making hand-cut noodles is the same. It's the combination of ingredients that makes the difference. A pasta cutter is a great investment if you plan on making noodles often, but cutting them with a knife by hand works just as well; it just takes a little extra time. (Please don't use a kunai knife for this—it might give your guests the wrong idea.)

TEUCHI UDON

LEVEL: CHŪNIN
PREP TIME: 1 HOUR PLUS 2 TO 8 HOURS RESTING TIME
COOK TIME: 30 MINUTES
YIELD: 4 SERVINGS

4 cups all-purpose flour

1 tablespoon salt

1¼ cup water, plus more as needed

1 egg yolk

Starch for dusting (cornstarch, potato starch, etc.)

Combine the flour and salt in a large bowl and mix well to combine.

Pour the contents out into the shape of a mound on your work surface, then use your fingers to make a small indentation in the middle.

Pour the water and egg yolk into the indentation, then work the liquid into the mixture using your hands. Depending on the flour, you may need to add more water; add just enough to get the flour to combine but not be too sticky.

Knead vigorously until the dough is smooth but firm, "like your earlobe" being the traditional Japanese guidance.

Roll the dough into a ball and wrap with plastic wrap, then set aside for at least 2 hours at room temperature or 8 hours in the fridge.

When ready to cut the noodles, unwrap the dough and place on a lightly floured work surface. Roll out into a rectangular shape ⅛ inch thick. Dust the top with starch, then, taking the short sides of the rectangle, fold them inward, as if you were folding a letter to fit in an envelope.

With the long side of the folded dough facing you, hold a sharp knife or cleaver perpendicular to the long side and cut the dough into strips ⅛ inch wide, resulting in thin, narrow strips when the pieces are unfolded.

Gently loosen the noodles to unfold them, then lightly dust with starch to prevent them from clumping. Divide them into four portions for easier cooking.

When ready to cook, bring a large pot of water to a boil, making sure there's enough water that the noodles won't be crowded and water can circulate freely. Add the noodles one portion at a time, waiting for the water to reach full boiling again before adding the next portion. Stir constantly to keep the noodles from sticking to the bottom. Once all the noodles are added to the water, cook for 2 to 3 more minutes.

Place a colander in the sink and carefully pour the contents of the pot into the colander, then rinse under cool or cold running water briefly to remove any surface starch.

Serve immediately in any recipe calling for cooked noodles.

SUBSTITUTION JUTSU: TEUCHI SOBA

LEVEL: CHŪNIN
PREP TIME: 3 HOURS
COOK TIME: 30 MINUTES
YIELD: 4 SERVINGS

¾ cup wheat flour
3¼ cups buckwheat flour
1 tablespoon salt
1¼ cup water, plus more as needed
Starch for dusting (cornstarch, potato starch, etc.)

To make buckwheat noodles, follow the same preparation and cooking instructions as for Teuchi Udon, replacing the ingredients with these instead. Mix the dry ingredients together before adding water.

SUBSTITUTION JUTSU: TEUCHI RAMEN

LEVEL: CHŪNIN
PREP TIME: 3 HOURS
COOK TIME: 30 MINUTES
YIELD: 4 SERVINGS

3¾ cups bread flour
1 teaspoon salt
1 teaspoon baking soda
2 teaspoons vital wheat gluten
1 cup water, plus more as needed
Starch for dustlng (cornstarch, potato starch, etc.)

To make ramen noodles, follow the same preparation and cooking instructions as for Teuchi Udon, replacing the ingredients with these instead. Mix the dry ingredients together before adding water.

SHUKAKU'S ONE-TAIL TANUKI SOBA

While he may have only one tail, the tanuki-like tailed beast of Hidden Sand Village is not a being to underestimate! He's destructive and belligerent, and even Gaara has had his struggles with him. But maybe all they needed to bond was a good bowl of noodles. Reminiscent of Shukaku's distinctive earthy coloring, this recipe uses colored tempura crumbles, called tenkasu, to bring a new twist on a classic noodle dish.

LEVEL: GENIN
PREP TIME: 20 MINUTES
COOK TIME: 20 MINUTES
YIELD: 4 SERVINGS
SPECIAL EQUIPMENT: KITCHEN THERMOMETER

FOR THE COLORED TENKASU

3 tablespoons all purpose flour

3 tablespoons water

Black food coloring

Vegetable oil for frying

FOR THE NOODLES

4 cups dashi

4 tablespoons soy sauce

3 tablespoons mirin

1 tablespoon sugar

2 servings cooked soba noodles

2 green onions, finely chopped

Shichimi togarashi for garnish

To make the tenkasu, combine the flour and water, then divide into two bowls. Add food coloring to one bowl to create a black batter.

Add a few cups of oil to a small pot over medium heat and bring to 350°F. Using a fork to scoop the batter, let the batter drip off the fork's tines and into the oil, creating batter droplets. Once the droplets float to the surface and start browning, remove from the oil and place on paper towels to drain. Continue frying until all the batter is used up.

To make the noodles, in a large pot, bring the dashi just to a boil over medium heat. Add the soy sauce, mirin, and sugar, then cook until the sugar is dissolved.

Place the noodles in serving bowls, then divide the broth between the bowls. Portion the tenkasu and green onions on top of both bowls, then sprinkle with shichimi togarashi to serve.

KURAMA'S NINE-TAILS KITSUNE UDON

It's rumored in Japan that aburaage is the favorite food of the fox (kitsune in Japanese). Tailed Beast or not, Kurama is still a kitsune at heart. Perhaps if Naruto had offered up some delicious aburaage at their first communication, their relationship would have gone more smoothly. This dish piles on the aburaage strips to make quite the tasty feast!

LEVEL: GENIN

PREP TIME: 10 MINUTES
COOK TIME: 10 MINUTES
YIELD: 4 SERVINGS

FOR THE SEASONED ABURAAGE

1 tablespoon soy sauce

2 tablespoons mirin

1 tablespoon sugar

½ cup dashi

2 aburaage rectangles

FOR THE NOODLES AND BROTH

4 cups dashi

4 tablespoons soy sauce

3 tablespoons mirin

1 tablespoon sugar

2 servings cooked udon

2 green onions, finely chopped

To prepare the seasoned aburaage, combine the soy sauce, mirin, sugar, and dashi in a small pot over medium heat. Add the aburaage, then let simmer until all the liquid has been absorbed. Let cool and set aside, then cut each rectangle into nine long strips.

In a large pot, bring the dashi just to a boil over medium heat. Add the soy sauce, mirin, and sugar, then cook until the sugar is dissolved.

Place the noodles in serving bowls, then divide the broth between the bowls. Arrange the strips of the aburaage on each bowl, fanned out from the center like Kurama's tails. Sprinkle with the green onions to serve.

NEJI'S HERRING SOBA

A member of the Hyūga branch house, Neji has a complex relationship with the main family. Resenting his role most of the time but accepting it in the end, he ultimately embraces tradition and serves his family well. This traditional soup is a comforting winter classic, especially popular in Kyoto, and probably in Konohagakure too. Perhaps it's Neji's favorite because it's a source of comfort he can enjoy without having to admit that he needs comforting. Fresh herring is best for the recipe, but canned or smoked herring works just as well.

LEVEL: GENIN
PREP TIME: 10 MINUTES
COOK TIME: 20 MINUTES
YIELD: 4 SERVINGS

FOR THE HERRING

8 shiitake mushrooms

1 cup dashi

⅓ cup sake

3 tablespoons sugar

⅓ cup mirin

⅓ cup soy sauce

4 herring fillets

FOR THE SOBA

2 bunches soba

½ cup soy sauce

½ cup mirin

2 cups dashi

2 green onions, chopped, for garnish

Prepare the herring by combining the mushrooms, dashi, sake, sugar, mirin, and soy sauce in a wide, shallow pot over medium-high heat. Once simmering, add the fillets and turn the heat down to low. Cover and let simmer for 20 minutes, taking care not to disturb the fillets too much so they don't lose their shape.

To prepare the soba, while the fillets are simmering, bring a large pot of water to a boil. Add the soba and let boil for 4 minutes, then strain the noodles immediately and place under running water until cooled off.

Heat the soy sauce, mirin, and dashi until it comes to a rolling boil to create the broth, then you're ready to serve! Place noodles into bowls, add the broth, then top with the herring, mushrooms, and green onions.

MIGHT GUY'S OVERFLOWING YOUTH SUPER-SPICY CURRY UDON

A master of taijutsu and a bottomless well of hard work and optimism . . . what's Guy's secret? Where does that energy come from? Perhaps his love for spicy curry holds the answer (and no doubt influenced Rock Lee's curry obsession as well).

LEVEL: GENIN
PREP TIME: 10 MINUTES
COOK TIME: 20 MINUTES
YIELD: 4 SERVINGS

4 servings freshly cooked udon

2 tablespoons neutral oil

1 small onion, thinly sliced lengthwise

2 tablespoons curry powder

4 cups dashi

½ cup mirin

½ cup soy sauce

1 tablespoon sugar

1 teaspoon yuzu kosho, or more to taste

1 teaspoon potato starch

1 pound beef, thinly sliced

3 cloves garlic, minced

2 green onions, thinly sliced

Shichimi togarashi

Cook the udon according to package directions, or follow the recipe (page 48) if making your own. Transfer to individual serving bowls and set aside.

Place the oil in a wide skillet over medium heat. When warm, add the onions and cook for about 10 minutes, until softened.

Meanwhile, place the curry powder in a small saucepan over medium heat. Cook until fragrant, turn the heat down to low, then slowly pour in the dashi, followed by the mirin, soy sauce, sugar, and yuzu kosho.

In a small bowl, combine the potato starch with a tablespoon of water and stir well to remove any clumps, then add to the pot and let simmer until it thickens, then remove from the heat and set aside.

Once the onions have cooked, add the beef and garlic and continue cooking for about 5 minutes more.

Add the curry sauce to the pan and stir to combine. Portion out the udon into four bowls, then ladle the curry mixture evenly between bowls. To serve, garnish with the green onions and add shichimi togarashi to taste.

SUBSTITUTION JUTSU
Want more heat? Load up on the yuzu kosho. Just don't go too far—you don't want to open all eight inner gates.

NARUTO'S INSTANT RAMEN HACKS

Growing up without parents, Naruto depended on instant ramen because he had to learn early in life how to cook for himself. Just because instant ramen is easy and fast, though, doesn't mean that it has to be boring! When you can't make it down to Ichiraku Ramen for a bowl, try these quick hacks to dress up your instant ramen into a gourmet meal. If you've eaten enough instant ramen, you know that the noodles get soggy if not eaten right away. So prepare the toppings first, then cook the noodles at the very end to maximize the dish's potential.

RAMEN TRANSFORMATION JUTSU #1: MISO-PORK FLAVOR VORTEX

LEVEL: GENIN
PREP TIME: 5 MINUTES
COOK TIME: 5 MINUTES
YIELD: 1 SERVING

1 tablespoon sesame oil

¼ pound ground pork

1 clove garlic, minced

¼ cup frozen corn

1 tablespoon miso

1 package instant ramen, any variety

Sliced green onion for garnish

Place a wide skillet over medium heat and add the oil. Once hot, add the pork and cook until browned, crumbling with a spoon as it cooks.

Add the garlic and cook until fragrant, then add the corn and continue cooking until the corn is just heated through.

Add the miso to the skillet and stir until the miso is fully incorporated, then remove from the heat and set aside.

Prepare the ramen according to package directions, including the broth and seasoning packets. Once cooked, place in the serving bowl, then ladle the prepared toppings on top. Garnish with green onions to serve.

RAMEN TRANSFORMATION JUTSU #2: ART OF THE MAGNIFICENT CHICKEN

LEVEL: GENIN
PREP TIME: 5 MINUTES
COOK TIME: 5 MINUTES
YIELD: 1 SERVING

1 tablespoon sesame oil

¼ pound shredded rotisserie chicken

1 clove garlic, minced

2 leaves napa cabbage, shredded

1 carrot, julienned

¼ inch fresh ginger, grated

1 tablespoon soy sauce

1 package instant ramen, any variety

1 nori sheet, cut into thin strips

Place a wide skillet over medium heat and add the oil. Once hot, add the chicken and cook until browned.

Add the garlic and cook until fragrant, then add the cabbage and carrot and continue cooking until softened.

Add the ginger and soy sauce to the skillet, stir until combined, then remove from the heat and set aside.

Prepare the ramen according to package directions, including the broth and seasoning packets. Once cooked, place in the serving bowl, then ladle the prepared toppings on top. Garnish with nori strips to serve.

RAMEN TRANSFORMATION JUTSU #3: ENDLESS POTATO CHEESE FLAVOR

LEVEL: GENIN
PREP TIME: 5 MINUTES
COOK TIME: 5 MINUTES
YIELD: 1 SERVING

1 tablespoon olive oil

1 strip bacon, chopped

1 clove garlic, minced

⅓ cup frozen shredded potato

1 slice swiss cheese

1 package instant ramen, any variety

Parsley for garnish

Place a wide skillet over medium heat and add the oil. Once hot, add the bacon and cook until browned.

Add the garlic and potatoes and cook until softened.

Pile all the ingredients toward the center of the pan, then turn off the heat and place the cheese on top and allow it to melt slightly.

Prepare the ramen according to package directions, including the broth and seasoning packets. Once cooked, place in the serving bowl, then use a spatula to transfer the prepared toppings on top. Garnish with parsley to serve.

SHADOW CLONE JUTSU: ICHIRAKU RAMEN

Naruto's favorite meal doesn't have to be limited to the Hidden Leaf Village! This classic ramen recipe will bring the aroma and flavor of Ichiraku from the Land of Fire right into your kitchen.

LEVEL: CHŪNIN
PREP TIME: 15 MINUTES, PLUS 12 HOURS TO MARINATE
COOK TIME: 3 HOURS
YIELD: 4 SERVINGS

SPECIAL EQUIPMENT

fine-mesh sieve

FOR THE EGGS (MAKE AT LEAST 12 HOURS IN ADVANCE)

1 cup soy sauce

½ cup sake

¼ cup mirin

2 cloves garlic, minced

1 green onion, chopped

½ inch fresh ginger, grated

4 large eggs

FOR THE BROTH

1 pound chicken bones

12 cups water

1 inch fresh ginger

3 cloves garlic

1 onion, roughly chopped

1 carrot, roughly chopped

1 cup soy sauce

¼ cup sake

¼ cup mirin

1 pound boneless pork shoulder

FOR THE CHASHU PORK

1 cup water

1 cup soy sauce

½ cup sake

¼ cup mirin

½ inch fresh ginger, grated

2 cloves garlic, minced

FOR THE DISH

4 portions freshly cooked ramen

4 ounces bamboo shoots

4 sheets nori, cut into squares

4 ounces narutomaki, sliced

4 green onions, thinly sliced

COOK-NIN NOTE: Getting ahold of chicken bones for this recipe doesn't have to be a hassle! If you buy chicken cuts with bones for other recipes, deboning them and storing the scraps in the freezer will give you an excuse to make plenty of ramen.

continues on page 60

Prepare the eggs ahead of time by combining the soy sauce, sake, mirin, garlic, green onion, and ginger in a small pot. Bring to a boil over high heat, then immediately remove from the heat and let cool.

While the sauce cools, fill a small pot with water and bring to a boil. When boiling, turn the heat down to low, add the eggs, still in their shells, then cover and let cook for 5 to 7 minutes. (Five minutes for the runniest of yolks!)

Once the eggs are cooked, drain immediately and place under running water to cool down. When cool to the touch, peel them and place in a small sealable container. Add the prepared sauce on top, then place in the fridge and let marinate for at least 12 hours.

To make the ramen, prepare the broth by rinsing the chicken bones under cold water, then placing in a large stock pot along with the water.

Add all the broth ingredients to the pot, placing the pork shoulder on top, then bring to a boil over high heat.

Once boiling, skim the surface to remove any scum and reduce the heat to low. Simmer uncovered for about 2 hours, until the water is reduced by half. Transfer the pork shoulder to a wide, shallow pot, then strain the broth through a fine-mesh sieve, transferring the liquid to a separate pot or bowl and discarding the remaining ingredients.

To finish the pork, add the chashu ingredients to the pot and bring to a boil over high heat.

When boiling, turn the heat down to low and let simmer for about 30 minutes, until the sauce has reduced in half. Transfer the pork from the pot to a cutting board and let rest for a few minutes before slicing.

To assemble, prepare four large bowls on your work surface, then bring a large pot of water to a boil over high heat. When boiling, add the ramen noodles and cook for about 3 minutes, until al dente. While the noodles are cooking, ladle the prepared broth into the bowls. Once the noodles are cooked, drain them into a colander, then portion them out into the bowls.

Arrange the pork, eggs, bamboo shoots, nori squares, and narutomaki on top of the bowls, garnish with green onions, and serve piping hot!

CHAPTER FOUR:
FISH AND SEAFOOD DISHES

While they may be in the heart of the Land of Fire, the love of fish runs deep in many Konoha shinobi, thanks in no small part to the Naka River, which flows through the Hidden Leaf Village, and the seafood sold at the Mohawk Fish Market. These recipes offer a variety of ways to satisfy anyone's fancy for fish.

KONOHAGAKURE ACADEMY
MISSION #4: LET'S MAKE FISH CAKES!

B-RANK

Being an island nation, it's no surprise that Japan has a variety of ways to cook with fish. Naruto and his allies are likewise quite familiar with fish and seafood dishes, thanks to their frequent ocean journeys. Which means skilled cook-nins must have some of these recipes in their repertoire, or find themselves lost at sea.

Fish cakes are a great place to start. You can buy them when convenient, but it's a great and rewarding challenge to make them yourself. The first recipe is Naruto's own namesake, the popular ramen topping called narutomaki. While there are many types of steamed fish cakes, collectively called kamaboko, narutomaki are a special variety with a pink spiral, named after the Naruto whirlpools in western Japan.

STEAMED FISH CAKES: NARUTOMAKI

LEVEL: CHŪNIN
PREP TIME: 15 MINUTES
COOK TIME: 15 MINUTES
YIELD: 8 SERVINGS
SPECIAL EQUIPMENT: FOOD PROCESSOR, SUSHI ROLLING MAT, BAMBOO STEAMER

8 ounces white fish fillets, such as pollock or cod

1 egg white

½ teaspoon salt

1 teaspoon sugar

1 teaspoon mirin

Red or pink food coloring

Remove the skin from the fillets if they have any, then place in a colander and thoroughly wash under cold running water. Pat dry with paper towels, pressing firmly to remove any excess water.

Roughly chop the fish and transfer to a food processor along with the egg white, salt, sugar, and mirin. Process until it becomes a fine paste.

Transfer one-third of the paste into a small bowl, then mix in the food coloring a drop or two at a time until a bright pink color is achieved.

Place a sheet of plastic wrap over the sushi mat, then use a spatula to spread the white paste on top of the wrap, forming a wide rectangle the height of the mat and about half the width, 9 inches by 5 inches. Spread the pink paste on top, leaving a ½-inch border along both 9-inch sides.

Starting at one of the longer sides, gently roll the paste up in a swiss roll, using the plastic to guide it, pulling away the plastic as you roll.

Once the paste is rolled, smooth out the seam, then use the freed plastic wrap to wrap the roll tightly. If the ends are not fully sealed, use a second sheet to wrap it fully, otherwise it may fall out while steaming. To finish, wrap it in a sushi mat, securing it with kitchen twine or rubber bands.

Place a 12-inch bamboo steamer over a wide pot filled with water. Bring to a boil over medium-high heat, then place the roll in and let steam for 15 minutes.

Let cool, then remove from the plastic wrap. Slice into ¼-inch rounds. If the sushi rolling mat did not leave enough imprint to create the flower-like indentations, you can use a knife to create more distinct curves on the edges. Serve on top of ramen and other noodle dishes.

FRIED FISH CAKES: SATSUMA-AGE

*These delightfully springy cakes have a subtle flavor,
making them the perfect pair for bold-flavored sauces.*

LEVEL: GENIN
PREP TIME: 15 MINUTES
COOK TIME: 15 MINUTES
YIELD: 12 SERVINGS
SPECIAL EQUIPMENT: FOOD PROCESSOR, KITCHEN THERMOMETER

1 pound white fish fillets

1 tablespoon sake

1 teaspoon salt

1 large egg

¼ cup julienned carrots

¼ cup thinly sliced green onions

Vegetable oil for frying

Cut the fillets into small, 1-inch cubes, then place in a food processor along with the sake and salt. Blend for a few seconds, then add the egg and blend until a smooth paste is formed.

Add the vegetables to the fish paste and mix until well blended.

Add about two inches of oil to a small pot over medium heat and bring to 350°F. While the oil is heating, use a spoon to scoop out the fish paste into twelve evenly portioned balls.

To fry the fish cakes, add two or three balls to the pot at a time and fry for about 3 minutes until golden brown, flipping them over as needed to evenly fry all sides. Remove with a slotted spoon and let drain on paper towels to remove any excess oil. Continue this process until all the balls have been fried.

Serve hot or at room temperature. If made a bit smaller, they are also a great addition to soups and noodle dishes in substitution for steamed fish cakes.

KAKASHI'S SALT-BROILED SAURY

Kakashi's signature White Light Chakra Sabre is unparalleled at delivering a series of cuts to the enemy. We suspect it also comes in handy with this fish recipe that he's said to favor! To eat it in true Japanese style, the bones should be removed with your chopsticks (not your fingers!), and placed toward the side of the plate as you eat. Remember this in case you're ever invited to dine with a village kage (looking at you, Naruto).

LEVEL: GENIN (OR JŌNIN, IF CLEANING THE FISH YOURSELF)
PREP TIME: 20 MINUTES
COOK TIME: 15 MINUTES
YIELD: 2 SERVINGS

2 whole Pacific saury

1 tablespoon salt

Grated daikon radish

1 lemon, cut into wedges

Soy sauce

Rinse the fish briefly under cool water, then pat dry thoroughly. Use your knife to cut a shallow slit lengthwise on either side of the fish, following the line formed by the coloration of the skin. Sprinkle the fish heavily on all sides with salt, then let sit for 15 minutes.

Preheat the oven on the broiler setting, on high, then place the saury on a baking sheet and place it directly under the broiler. Let cook for 8 to 10 minutes on each side, turning the fish over once a nice char develops on the skin.

To serve, plate each fish alongside individual small bowls of grated daikon, lemon, and soy sauce.

PREPARATORY JUTSU: INSIDE-OUTSIDE PRECISE SLICE TECHNIQUE

Saury can be enjoyed whole, and many Japanese enjoy the contrast of the bitter taste of the intestines, but they can also be removed before cooking. To do so, first create a ¼-inch-deep cut under the head of the fish, just until it reaches the vertebra. Next, make a shallow cut at the back of the stomach, just in front of the anal vent. Bend the head to the side with your hands and pull it out, and the intestines should slide right out with it. If not, you can make a shallow cut along the stomach to slice it open, then remove the intestines. (You could also buy the fish already cleaned, or ask your fishmonger to do this, but what self-respecting shinobi passes up a chance to practice their knife work?)

SEA MONSTER TEMPURA

A versatile technique that works well with a wide variety of fish (and vegetables, meats, and pretty much anything else), this tempura recipe will give you perfection in fried form.

LEVEL: CHŪNIN
PREP TIME: 15 MINUTES
COOK TIME: 15 MINUTES
YIELD: 4 SERVINGS
SPECIAL EQUIPMENT: KITCHEN THERMOMETER

FOR THE DIPPING SAUCE

¾ cup dashi

2 tablespoons soy sauce

2 tablespoons mirin

1 tablespoon sugar

FOR THE FISH

1 pound white-fleshed fish fillets (flounder, cod, snapper, etc.)

¼ cup starch (cornstarch, potato starch, etc.)

Vegetable oil for frying

1 egg yolk

1 cup cold water

¼ cup ice cubes

1½ cups cake flour

To prepare the sauce, combine the dashi, soy sauce, mirin, and sugar in a small pot over high heat and bring to a boil. Once boiling, turn off heat and let cool.

Prepare the fish by cutting it into bite-size pieces. If using fillets with skin, make shallow parallel cuts on the skin side about ¼ inch apart to help prevent fish from curling while frying.

Pat the fillets dry with paper towels, then coat generously with the starch and set aside.

Place a few inches of oil in a wide pot over medium heat and bring to 350°F. While the oil is heating, place the egg yolk, water, and ice cubes in a small bowl and whisk well to combine.

Prepare your work station by setting a paper towel–lined tray to one side of the stove, and place the fish and the flour within reach.

When the oil is hot, add the flour to the egg mixture and stir for about 20 seconds, until roughly combined. It's OK if there are still some flour clumps in the batter; you just want it mostly mixed up.

It's critical to keep the oil temperature steady for the right texture, so fry only a few pieces at a time. Working with one fish piece at a time, quickly dip the fish in the batter, then immediately add it to the oil, letting it fry for a few seconds before adding another piece to the pan.

Fry for about 3 to 5 minutes, depending on the size of the pieces, until golden brown. Remove from the pan using a slotted spoon, then transfer to the paper towel–lined plate to drain. Between batches, skim and discard the crumbs left behind in the oil (or save them as a topping for some Soba, see page 51).

Serve with Shuriken Senbei (page 27) to honor the epic battle that Naruto and the other shinobi fought against the giant marlin from the Third Shinobi World War.

COOK-NIN NOTE: Keep everything cold! Cold bowl, ice cold water; make the batter just before cooking. Don't overstir the batter, otherwise the gluten will develop and you'll end up with a chewier texture.

EIGHT-TAILS TAKO SU

An octopus-like creature of epic proportions, Gyūki is a behemoth of a tailed beast with enormous chakra to match. His tentacles can be used as a medium for his chakra when severed, but there's no such risk of such injury with this recipe. However, if your diners haven't eaten octopus before, they may react as if this refreshing salad is some kind of yōkai!

LEVEL: GENIN
PREP TIME: 15 MINUTES
YIELD: 4 SERVINGS

3 tablespoons rice vinegar

1 tablespoon sugar

1 tablespoon soy sauce

¼ inch fresh ginger, grated

½ tablespoon dried wakame

1 small cucumber

1 teaspoon salt

¼ pound boiled (precooked) octopus, sliced

Combine the rice vinegar, sugar, soy sauce, and ginger in a small bowl and stir to combine, then set aside.

Place the wakame in a small bowl of water and let sit for 15 minutes to allow the wakame to rehydrate.

Slice the cucumber thinly and place in a small bowl. Stir in the salt, and let it sit for 15 minutes.

Gently squeeze out the water from the cucumbers with your hands, taking a handful at a time and squeezing it between your palms, then place in a large bowl.

Add the sliced octopus, wakame, and seasoning and stir well to combine.

Serve chilled.

SHIKAMARU'S SIMMERED MACKEREL

Cooking? What a drag! When it comes to preparing a meal (and everything else), Shikamaru's philosophy leans toward easier is better, and it doesn't get much easier than simmering some fish away in a pan. Just don't get so caught up in a game of shogi that you forget to eat the fish when it's done!

LEVEL: GENIN
PREP TIME: 5 MINUTES
COOK TIME: 20 MINUTES
YIELD: 4 SERVINGS

1 pound mackerel fillets, with skin

1 cup sake

2 tablespoons grated fresh ginger

2 tablespoons soy sauce

2 tablespoons mirin

1 cup dashi

2 tablespoons miso

1 cup grated daikon radish

3 green onions, finely chopped

Shichimi togarashi

Pat dry the mackerel fillets, then cut into four roughly 3-inch pieces.

Place the sake and ginger in a wide saucepan, then stir to distribute. Lay the fish skin side down in the pan, making sure the pieces don't overlap. Bring to a boil over high heat, then cover and reduce heat to medium low. Let simmer for 10 minutes.

Combine the soy sauce, mirin, dashi, and miso in a small bowl. Remove the lid of the saucepan and add the mixture. Let simmer uncovered until the liquid has reduced by half.

Spread the radish on top of the fillets, then sprinkle with the green onion. Replace the lid and let simmer 2 minutes more, just enough to let the green onions soften.

Using a spatula, carefully transfer the fillets to individual shallow bowls, taking care to ensure that the radish and onion do not fall off. Spoon a bit of the sauce on top of each fillet, then serve immediately, sprinkled with shichimi togarashi as desired.

KISAME'S CHIRASHI SUSHI

Having difficulty mastering your sushi-rolling jutsu? No problem! Sushi rolls may be popular, but there are many ways to enjoy sushi rice in Japan. Chirashi sushi, or scattered sushi, is a quick and easy sushi dish enjoyed at home and is just the thing to highlight some of Kisame's favorite fish!

LEVEL: GENIN
PREP TIME: 10 MINUTES, PLUS 30 MINUTES FOR SOAKING THE MUSHROOMS
COOK TIME: 20 MINUTES
YIELD: 4 SERVINGS

FOR THE RICE

2 dried shiitake mushrooms

1 carrot, julienned

1 block aburaage, thinly sliced

⅓ cup water

2 tablespoons sugar

¼ cup rice vinegar

2 cups freshly cooked rice

FOR THE CREPES

2 large eggs

1 tablespoon dashi

1 teaspoon mirin

¼ teaspoon salt

FOR TOPPINGS

4 ounces cooked crabmeat

½ cup shrimp, cooked and peeled

4 ounces narutomaki, sliced

4 snow peas, halved

1 sheet nori, thinly sliced

1 tablespoon sesame seeds

To start the rice, soak the mushrooms in warm water until softened, about 30 minutes. Cut them into small strips, then place in a small pot over medium heat along with the carrot, aburaage, water, and sugar. Let the mixture simmer until the carrot has softened, about 5 minutes, then remove from the heat and let cool.

To make the crepes, place the eggs, dashi, mirin, and salt in a small bowl and whisk to combine. Place a nonstick pan over medium heat and, once hot, pour a thin layer of egg in the pan, then cover with a tight-fitting lid and let cook for a few minutes until set. Remove from the pan and place on a cutting board to cool, then continue cooking more thin layers until all the egg is used up. Once cooled, slice the egg into narrow strips.

Finish the rice by adding the rice vinegar to the cooled vegetable mixture, then pouring the mixture into a large bowl along with the cooked rice. Use a rice paddle or spatula to gently fold the vegetables into the rice, stirring until all the grains are evenly coated and glossy.

To assemble, place the seasoned rice in a wide, shallow serving bowl (or a wooden hangiri, if you're feeling fancy), then arrange the egg strips on top. Layer on the crabmeat, shrimp, narutomaki, and snow peas, then top with the nori and sesame seeds.

CHAPTER FIVE: MEAT DISHES

When it comes to protein, meat is supreme! Whether it be Chōji's
love of yakiniku, or Kiba's fondness for dog food, each shinobi has their
favorite meat dish to power them through their toughest training days.

KONOHAGARUKE ACADEMY
MISSION #5: LET'S MAKE CHICKEN TERIYAKI!

When it comes to Japanese meat dishes, there's none quite as world-renowned as chicken teriyaki. We tend to associate teriyaki with a flavor, but in Japan, it's actually more of a technique, its name derived from the Japanese words *teri* (to shine) and *yaki* (to broil or grill). To be true teriyaki, the food just needs to look glossy and grilled! Leaving the skin on is critical for authentic flavor, and you may find that with the right pan, you don't even need oil to achieve some beautiful browning on the chicken. Skip the bottled stuff and make your own teriyaki sauce with just a few standard ingredients!

CLASSIC CHICKEN TERIYAKI

LEVEL: CHŪNIN
PREP TIME: 10 MINUTES
COOK TIME: 10 MINUTES
YIELD: 4 SERVINGS

8 chicken thighs, skin on, bone removed

4 tablespoons soy sauce

2 tablespoons mirin

2 tablespoons sugar

2 tablespoons rice vinegar

½ inch fresh ginger, grated

1 tablespoon vegetable oil or olive oil

2 cups shredded cabbage

Combine the chicken, soy sauce, mirin, sugar, rice vinegar, and ginger in a small bowl and set aside.

Place a wide skillet over medium-high heat and add the oil. When hot, remove the chicken from the sauce and add it, skin side down, to the pan. Cook for about 4 minutes, until the skin turns golden. Flip the chicken and cook for another 4 minutes, until the chicken is almost cooked through.

Add the sauce, shaking the pan gently to distribute it, then cover with a tight-fitting lid and let steam for 1 minute. Remove the lid, then let simmer until the sauce has reduced. Turn the chicken to coat it in the sauce, then remove from the pan and let rest on a cutting board for a few minutes.

To serve, cut each thigh into thin strips and serve alongside the cabbage.

CHŌJI'S YAKINIKU

Whether it be a successful mission, a new jutsu mastered, or just because, Chōji's favorite way to celebrate is with a special feast! (His sensei Asuma has learned how effective a food reward can be in motivating Chōji.) Yakiniku is a unique social experience for shinobi teams, or any group of friends: a chance to cook and bond together at the table. Considering how much yakiniku Team Asuma eats, their bond must be unbreakable!

LEVEL: GENIN
PREP TIME: 40 MINUTES, PLUS 1 HOUR TO REST SAUCE
COOK TIME: 15 MINUTES
YIELD: 6 SERVINGS
SPECIAL EQUIPMENT: SHICHIRIN OR OTHER SMALL GRILL (OPTIONAL)

FOR THE SAUCE (PREPARE IN ADVANCE, OVERNIGHT IF POSSIBLE)

2 tablespoons dashi

2 tablespoons mirin

3 tablespoons soy sauce

1 tablespoon sugar

1 teaspoon rice vinegar

1 tablespoon plain applesauce

1 tablespoon toasted white sesame seeds

FOR THE MEAT AND VEGETABLES

2 pounds assorted grilling meat (excellent choices are rib-eye, flank, sirloin, tenderloin, pork belly, chicken breast)

2 cups sliced assorted vegetables (mushroom, onion, carrot, squash, eggplant)

2 cups shredded cabbage

1 tablespoon salt

Lemon for serving

Prepare the sauce by combining all the ingredients in a small pan and bringing to a boil over high heat. Once boiling, turn the heat off and let cool down, then transfer to a sealable container and let sit in the fridge for at least 1 hour, preferably overnight.

To prepare the meat and vegetables, first chill the meat in the freezer for about 30 minutes to make it easier to cut, then slice into ¼-inch strips.

Prepare the shredded cabbage by placing it in a large bowl of cold water and adding the salt. Let it sit for about 30 minutes, then drain well and let dry.

To cook, preheat the oven broiler. While the oven is warming, prepare the table by portioning out the cabbage on individual plates and preparing individual dipping bowls for the sauce.

Line a rimmed baking sheet with foil, and if you have a small wire rack, place on top of the foil to help with even cooking.

Cook in batches, starting with the vegetables, cooking for about 1 minute per side until the desired doneness is achieved. If the meat is well marbled, the pieces can be cooked as is, but drier ingredients may benefit from a spritz of oil. Transfer cooked items to a serving tray as they're done and continue with the remaining ingredients.

For peak flavor, the diners can be served the food as it comes out of the oven, but it can also be served all together when everything's done at the end.

Enjoy by dipping the grilled ingredients in the prepared sauce, or even just sprinkling with a squeeze of lemon or a little salt.

COOK-NIN NOTE: This recipe calls for cooking with the oven's broiler setting, but to be really authentic, you can buy a tabletop Japanese grill, called a shichirin, online. A regular charcoal grill, or even a small gas grill used for camping, works just as well (be sure to follow all guidelines for safety).

AKIMICHI CLAN CHANKO NABE

With all the calorie-intensive jutsus used by the Akimichi clan, they really need to eat! Following in the tradition of Japanese sumo, this filling dish is the preferred hotpot of sumo wrestlers, as well as shinobi in training!

LEVEL: GENIN
PREP TIME: 20 MINUTES
COOK TIME: 15 MINUTES
YIELD: 6 SERVINGS

FOR THE PONZU DIPPING SAUCE

¼ cup soy sauce

2 tablespoons lemon juice

2 tablespoons mirin

1 tablespoon rice vinegar

¼ teaspoon instant dashi granules

FOR THE SESAME DIPPING SAUCE

¼ cup tahini

2 tablespoons soy sauce

2 tablespoon mirin

2 tablespoons rice vinegar

2 tablespoons sugar

1 tablespoon miso paste

¼ teaspoon instant dashi granules

1 tablespoon toasted sesame seeds

FOR THE HOTPOT

1 bunch green onions, divided

½ pound ground chicken

1 large egg

1 inch fresh ginger

1 tablespoon soy sauce

1 tablespoon cornstarch

1 package harusame noodles

6 shiitake mushrooms

6 cups dashi

¼ cup sake

¼ cup mirin

½ cup miso

½ pound thinly sliced pork

½ pound boneless, skinless chicken thighs, cut into 1-inch cubes

1 carrot, sliced into ¼-inch disks

1 package tofu (about 400 grams, or 14 ounces), cut into 1-inch cubes

½ head napa cabbage, cut into 2-inch chunks

FOR THE ZOSUI

2 cups freshly cooked rice

1 large egg, beaten

continues on page 80

Prepare one or both of the sauces by combining all the ingredients for each in a small bowl. Set in the fridge until ready to use.

Prepare the meatballs for the hotpot by finely chopping two of the green onions, then placing them in a medium bowl and adding the ground chicken, egg, ginger, soy sauce, and cornstarch. Mix very well, then set aside.

Cut the remaining green onions into 2-inch strips and set aside. Prepare the noodles and mushrooms by placing both in bowls of water and letting them rehydrate for a few minutes.

To start the broth for the hotpot, combine the dashi, sake, and mirin in a dutch oven or wide pot over medium heat. When warm, spoon several ladlefuls into a small bowl and add the miso. Stir until the miso is dissolved, then return it to the pot and turn the heat down to medium low. Do not let the broth boil after this point!

To cook the hotpot, start by taking spoonfuls of the ground chicken mixture and shaping it into balls, then add them to the pot, stirring between each addition to make sure they don't stick to the pot. Move them to the side of the pot, and for each new addition, nestle the ingredient in a specific spot in the pot so all the ingredients stay organized. There is no need to stir the pot after this point. Add the pork and chicken thighs, cover, and let cook for about 8 minutes.

Remove the lid and add the carrot, shiitake, and tofu, then cook for about 5 minutes more. A few minutes before serving, add the harusame, cabbage, and remaining green onion and cook just until softened, then transfer the pot to the table.

To serve, allow each person to ladle their own servings into their own bowl, and prepare individual dipping bowls on the side.

As an after-dinner treat, when the hotpot is finished, you can end the meal Japanese style, with a nice bowl of zosui! Add the rice and egg to the pot, then cover and let it cook over medium-low heat for a few minutes until thickened, adding a bit more water as needed.

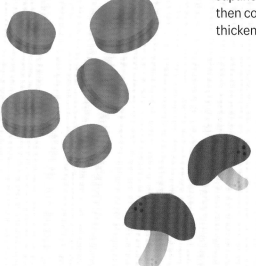

SHADOW CLONE JUTSU: BORUTO'S GREEN CHILE HAMBURGERS

Like father, like son. As much as Naruto loves his ramen, Boruto loves his burgers! One stands out among the rest: the spicy green chile burger. Choose your chiles for this recipe based on your desired spiciness. Hatch chiles or jalapeños are excellent candidates for spicier options.

LEVEL: GENIN
PREP TIME: 10 MINUTES
COOK TIME: 20 MINUTES
YIELD: 6 SERVINGS

1 pound ground beef

1 teaspoon salt

¼ teaspoon pepper

1 cup green chiles

1 tablespoon neutral oil

1 avocado

6 hamburger buns

6 slices pepper Jack cheese

6 leaves lettuce (iceberg or romaine are good)

1 tomato, sliced

½ white onion, finely diced

Combine the ground beef, salt, and pepper in a medium bowl. Mix well with your hands to combine, then set aside.

Meanwhile, prepare the chiles by first preheating the oven with the broiler set on high. Cut the tops off the peppers, then halve them and remove the seeds. Place on an aluminum foil–lined baking sheet, brush with the oil, and broil for about 7 minutes, until lightly charred. Remove from the oven and let cool.

Prepare the avocado by scooping out the pulp and placing it in a small bowl. Mash with a fork, then set aside.

To cook the burgers, place a wide skillet over medium heat. While it's heating up, shape the burgers by dividing the hamburger mixture into six portions. Flatten each into a disk, then gently toss the patty back and forth between your hands, as if you were playing with a hot potato, to help firm up the burger surface.

Once the skillet is hot, first toast the hamburger buns by adding a small amount of oil to the pan and placing the cut sides of the buns on the pan's surface. Cook until lightly toasted, then remove from the heat and set aside, toasted side up, to prevent them from getting soggy.

Next, cook the burgers by adding them to the pan. Cook until browned on one side, then flip over and continue cooking to the desired doneness, pressing the burger flat with the spatula every so often. Right before removing from the skillet, place the cheese slices on top and let warm slightly, then remove from the heat.

To assemble, spread a little avocado mash on the top of the bun and then, starting from the bottom bun, layer the lettuce, tomato, hamburger, chiles, and onions, finishing with the top bun.

SUBSTITUTION JUTSU: RICE BURGER BUNS

Leave it to Japan to find a way to bring together rice and burgers! As a bonus, these rice buns not only have a fresh-bread flavor, but they're also gluten-free.

LEVEL: CHŪNIN
PREP TIME: 10 MINUTES
COOK TIME: 20 MINUTES
YIELD: 6 BUNS

3 cups freshly cooked Japanese rice
½ tablespoon cornstarch
½ teaspoon salt
2 tablespoons neutral oil

Combine the rice, cornstarch, and salt in a medium bowl and stir well to combine. Place a bowl of water nearby to help keep your hands wet. Divide the mixture into twelve equal portions, then use your hands or a cookie cutter to flatten them out into equal-size disks. Press firmly with your hands to ensure the rice sticks together, and rinse off your hands when the rice starts getting too sticky.

Heat the oil on a large nonstick skillet over medium-high heat. Carefully place the rice patties on the surface, then cook on each side for about 10 minutes, until the rice starts to brown. Flip and continue cooking on the other side until browned as well.

Let cool slightly, then serve immediately in substitution for regular hamburger buns.

SHADOW CLONE JUTSU: SUPER-SOUR BURGER

Another favorite burger often found on Boruto's plate is the Super-Sour Burger, though not everyone he shares it with is as enthusiastic. What's the secret ingredient? Lemons, and lots of them! Lightning Burger serves it with the whole lemon, rind and all, and the secret to this recipe is pickling the lemon beforehand. That may take a few weeks, but it's worth the wait.

LEVEL: GENIN
PREP TIME: 15 MINUTES, PLUS 2 WEEKS TO PICKLE
COOK TIME: 15 MINUTES
YIELD: 6 SERVINGS

FOR THE PICKLED LEMONS

8 large lemons (Meyer or other thinner-rind varieties are best)

½ cup salt

1 tablespoon sugar

1½ cups fresh lemon juice

FOR THE BURGERS

1 pound ground beef

1 teaspoon salt

¼ teaspoon pepper

1 tablespoon neutral oil

6 hamburger buns

1 cup shredded lettuce

FOR THE LEMON AIOLI

½ cup mayonnaise

2 tablespoons lemon juice

2 cloves garlic, minced

1 teaspoon Dijon mustard

To make the pickled lemons, slice the lemons into ¼-inch slices, then transfer them to a large bowl and mix with the salt and sugar. Let sit for about 1 hour to let the moisture start getting pulled out of the lemons.

Transfer the lemon mixture to a small sealable container, then press down firmly to make sure they're settled in the container. Add enough lemon juice to just cover the lemons, then transfer to the fridge and let them pickle for at least two weeks.

When the lemons are ready, prepare the burgers by combining the ground beef, salt, and pepper in a medium bowl. Mix well with your hands to combine, then set aside for at least 15 minutes.

Prepare the aioli by mixing all the ingredients in a small bowl, then set it in the fridge until ready to use.

To cook the burgers, place a wide skillet over medium heat. While it's heating up, shape the burgers by dividing the hamburger mixture into six portions. Flatten each into a disk, then gently toss the patty back and forth between your hands, as if you were playing with a hot potato, to help firm up the burger surface.

Once the skillet is hot, first toast the hamburger buns by adding the oil to the pan and placing the cut sides of the buns on the pan's surface. Cook until lightly toasted, then remove from the heat and set aside, toasted side up, to prevent them from getting soggy.

Place the burgers in the pan and cook until browned on one side, then flip over and continue cooking to the desired doneness, pressing the burger flat with the spatula every so often.

To assemble, spread a little aioli on both buns, then layer the hamburger, lemons, and lettuce, finishing with the top bun.

SAKURA'S UMEBOSHI CHICKEN

A little bit salty, a little bit sweet, the unique flavor profile of this recipe is a balance of boldness and grace, much like Sakura herself.

LEVEL: GENIN
PREP TIME: 15 MINUTES
COOK TIME: 15 MINUTES
YIELD: 4 SERVINGS

2 chicken breasts, cut into 1-inch cubes

1 tablespoon umeboshi paste (from 2 large umeboshi)

1 inch fresh ginger

2 tablespoons olive oil

3 cloves garlic, minced

2 tablespoon soy sauce

2 tablespoons sake

2 tablespoons dashi

1 tablespoon mirin

1 tablespoon sugar

1 teaspoon potato starch

Toasted sesame seeds for garnish

To prepare the chicken, combine the umeboshi paste and ginger in a small bowl. Add the chicken and stir to coat. Let marinate for about 15 minutes.

When ready to cook, heat the oil in a wide skillet over medium heat. Add the garlic and cook until fragrant, then add the chicken mixture and cook for about 8 minutes, until the chicken is almost cooked through, stirring occasionally as the bottoms brown.

While the chicken is cooking, prepare the sauce by combining the soy sauce, sake, dashi, mirin, sugar, and potato starch in a small bowl. When the chicken is ready, add the sauce to the pan and cook for about 5 minutes more, until the sauce has reduced to a thick paste.

Serve sprinkled with toasted sesame seeds.

INFINITE TSUKUYOMI TSUKUNE

While the Infinite Tsukuyomi might be powerful enough to trap the whole world in an illusion, the only genjutsu you'll have to worry about while eating these chicken meatballs is getting lost in a world of flavor.

LEVEL: CHŪNIN
PREP TIME: 10 MINUTES
COOK TIME: 40 MINUTES
YIELD: 4 SERVINGS
SPECIAL EQUIPMENT: BAMBOO SKEWERS

FOR THE SWEET-AND-SOUR SAUCE

1 cup pineapple juice

½ cup packed brown sugar

⅓ cup rice vinegar

3 tablespoons ketchup

2 tablespoons soy sauce

1 tablespoon cornstarch

1 tablespoon black sesame seeds

FOR THE TSUKUNE

1 pound ground chicken

1 small onion, grated

1 inch fresh ginger, grated

3 cloves garlic, minced

1 large egg

½ cup breadcrumbs

Sesame oil

Prepare the bamboo skewers by placing them in a shallow bowl of water, then set aside until ready to use.

To make the sauce, combine the pineapple juice, brown sugar, vinegar, ketchup, and soy sauce in a small pan, then bring to a boil over high heat.

Once boiling, reduce the heat to low. Mix the cornstarch with a tablespoon or so of water to make a slurry, then add it to the pan and stir to combine. Let the sauce simmer for about 5 minutes, until it has thickened, then add the sesame seeds, remove from the heat, and set aside.

Preheat the oven by turning the broiler on high.

To prepare the tsukune, combine the ground chicken, onion, ginger, garlic, egg, and breadcrumbs in a small bowl. Knead with your hands for several minutes, an important step to help keep the meat on the skewer.

To shape, lightly coat your hands with sesame oil, then take a large spoonful of the mixture in your hands. Shape into a ball, then toss lightly from one hand to the other several times to help firm up the surface.

To grill, skewer two to four meatballs on each bamboo skewer, then cover the remaining wood with aluminum foil to prevent it from burning. Brush the surface with oil, then place on a greased rimmed baking sheet. Place directly under the broiler, then cook for 3 minutes per side, rotating them as each side finishes cooking, until a nice char develops on the surface. Remove from the oven and brush with the sauce, then return to the oven to broil for a few minutes more before serving.

AKAMARU'S FAVORITE DOG FOOD

Kiba provides nothing but the best for his furry best friend, which could be the reason why Akamaru grew from a tiny puppy into a canine big enough for Kiba to ride on! Scrambled ground meat, called soboro in Japanese, is a dish that's easy to prepare, has a great nutritional blend, and is perfect for all ninja, whether dog or human. Omit any seasoning and sauces when cooking for your own ninja dogs, but if cooking this recipe for people, you may find that an extra drizzle of soy sauce or even a dab of miso can enhance the dish.

LEVEL: GENIN
PREP TIME: 10 MINUTES
COOK TIME: 30 MINUTES
YIELD: 4 SERVINGS

3 large eggs

1 teaspoon salt

2 tablespoons sesame oil, divided

1 pound ground chicken

½ inch fresh ginger, grated

2 tablespoons mirin

2 tablespoons soy sauce

1 cup frozen peas

4 servings freshly cooked rice

Whisk the eggs in a small bowl with the salt. Set aside for 10 minutes. (This helps transform the egg proteins and makes the eggs firmer.)

Place a wide skillet over medium heat. When hot, add 1 tablespoon of sesame oil, then add the eggs and cook until fully set, stirring constantly to create finely scrambled eggs. Remove from the pan and set aside.

Place the remaining 1 tablespoon of oil in the pan, then add the chicken, crumbling it apart with a spatula as it cooks. Cook for about 8 minutes, until mostly cooked through, then add the ginger, mirin, and soy sauce. Let cook for about 5 more minutes, until all the moisture has been evaporated. Remove from the heat and set aside.

Place a small pot of water over high heat and bring to a boil. Once boiling, add the peas and cook for about 3 minutes until parboiled, then drain in a colander and let cool.

To assemble, place the rice in four individual serving bowls. Place the scrambled egg on top of half of the rice, then place the scrambled chicken on the other. Arrange the peas down the middle of the bowls to serve.

CHAPTER SIX:
VEGETABLE DISHES

The Land of Vegetables might be a minor country in Naruto's world, but in a healthy diet, veggies should be a major player! These recipes make great sides, adding flavorful nutrition to any meal, and they make refreshing snacks as well.

KONOHAGAKURE ACADEMY MISSION #6: LET'S MAKE JAPANESE-STYLE PICKLES!

C-RANK

For a truly authentic Japanese meal, you need only a few things: rice, miso soup, and pickles. Yes, pickles! But pickling doesn't have to be a long, intensive process. Even lightly pickling vegetables for a refreshing, crisp bite can provide a simple, satisfying side dish for any meal of the day. As a bonus, pickled vegetables last longer than fresh ones when you're on a far-flung mission.

QUICK PICKLED CUCUMBER

LEVEL: GENIN
PREP TIME: 15 MINUTES
YIELD: 4 SERVINGS
SPECIAL EQUIPMENT: MANDOLINE

1 large cucumber

1 inch fresh ginger

1 tablespoon salt

Using a mandoline or the slit side of a box grater, slice cucumber into thin strips. Use one of the finer sides to grate the ginger into a pulp.

Combine all the ingredients together in a small bowl, gently massaging it together to press the salt into the cucumber. Let sit for at least 15 minutes.

Use your hands to gently squeeze the cucumbers to remove excess moisture. Serve chilled or at room temperature.

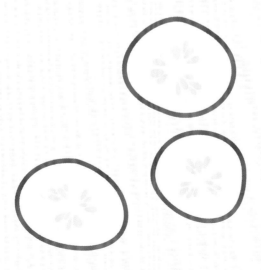

YAMANAKA FLOWERS' CHRYSANTHEMUM RADISHES

While Ino and Sakura may fight over who can bring Sasuke flowers, Ino knows the real secret to impressing a boy: bringing him food! Her solution is edible flowers, or edible vegetables shaped like flowers. These garnishes may even become hot sellers at Yamanaka Flowers.

LEVEL: JŌNIN
PREP TIME: 40 MINUTES , PLUS 24 HOURS TO PICKLE
COOK TIME: 5 MINUTES
YIELD: 12 SERVINGS

½ cup rice vinegar

½ cup dashi

2 tablespoons sugar

1 pound small radishes

4 cups water

¼ cup salt

Mix the rice vinegar, dashi, and sugar in a small pan and bring to a simmer over medium-high heat. Once the sugar has dissolved, remove from the heat and let cool.

Prepare your radishes by first cutting off the bottom to make a flat base. Place two chopsticks parallel to each other on your work surface, then place the radish between them. Using the chopsticks as a buffer to prevent you from cutting too deeply (don't use your good chopsticks, in case you make a few nicks in them!), make narrow vertical cuts down the length of the radishes, creating thin slices about ⅛ inch thick.

Once you've cut down the length of the radish, rotate it 90 degrees and repeat the process down the other side. You basically want to make a crosshatch pattern of cuts.

When all the radishes have been cut, combine the water and salt, and once the salt has completely dissolved, place the cut radishes in it. Let them sit for about 30 minutes to help them soften.

continues on page 96

After about 30 minutes, the "petals" will be pretty flexible. Remove the radishes, gently squeeze out excess water from each one, then place them in a jar or plastic container. Pour the vinegar mixture over the radishes and let them pickle for at least 30 minutes, up to 24 hours. Use a container that allows the radishes to be mostly covered by the liquid, but if needed, pour equal amounts of water and vinegar into the container until they are just submerged.

The color from the skin will slowly penetrate the rest of the radish over time. After about 24 hours, the pink will have subtly blended into the outermost leaves. If you want the color to be completely even, let them sit for two to three days. The pickles keep in the fridge for at least a week, so they're perfect for pulling a flower or two out for each meal to have a delicate accent all week long!

COOK-NIN NOTE: Ready to go big? Japanese chefs will make larger versions of this recipe by using daikon radish, but the technique is the same. Just cut a 2-inch disk from a daikon and repeat the process!

SASUKE'S SOY-PICKLED TOMATOES

It's a little-known fact that Sasuke loves tomatoes. Maybe it has to do with fond memories of growing them with Itachi and Fugaku, or maybe it's because they're just so delicious. Maybe all those tomatoes in the Uchiha diet is what led to the red color of their Sharingan!

LEVEL: CHŪNIN
PREP TIME: 5 MINUTES, PLUS 12 HOURS TO MARINATE
COOK TIME: 5 MINUTES
YIELD: 4 SERVINGS

2 to 3 large tomatoes

⅔ cup dashi

1 cup rice vinegar

3 tablespoons sugar

2 tablespoons soy sauce

1 teaspoon salt

Prepare the tomatoes by bringing a large pot of water to a boil. Remove the stems from the tomatoes, then cut a shallow cross mark on the bottom of each. Add them to the water, then let boil for about 30 seconds, flip, and boil for 30 seconds more. Immediately remove the tomatoes from the pot and place them under running water to cool down.

While the tomatoes cool off, prepare the pickling jar. Add the dashi, vinegar, sugar, soy sauce, and salt to a small pot and bring to a boil. Stir until the sugar is melted, then remove from the heat and let cool.

Once the tomatoes are cool, gently remove the skin by peeling at the corners of the cross marks. The skin should come away easily, but you can rub at it gently with your fingers to loosen it. Transfer the tomatoes to a small sealable container, then pour the pickling liquid on top.

Seal the container, then place in the fridge to marinate for at least 12 hours. Slice the tomatoes to serve.

SAI'S ARTFUL AGEDASHI TOFU

You may not possess the artistic sensibility that allows Sai to bring his ink drawings to life, but in his honor you can enjoy decorating these savory tofu blocks with a sauce of edible ink.

LEVEL: CHŪNIN
PREP TIME: 15 MINUTES
COOK TIME: 20 MINUTES
YIELD: 4 SERVINGS
SPECIAL EQUIPMENT: KITCHEN THERMOMETER, PLASTIC SQUEEZE BOTTLE

1 package firm tofu (about 400 grams, or 14 ounces)

2 tablespoons soy sauce

2 tablespoons mirin

2 tablespoons sake

2 cups dashi

Vegetable oil for frying

½ cup potato starch for dusting

Green onions, finely chopped, for garnish

Grated daikon radish for garnish

Remove the tofu from its container, drain briefly, then cut into eight blocks of equal size. To help the tofu firm up, place a few paper towels on the bottom of a baking sheet, then evenly space the tofu on top. Lay a few more paper towels on top of the tofu, then place another baking sheet or a cutting board on top to serve as a tofu press. (You can even place a bowl or another small weight on top to add a little extra pressure.) Leave to drain for about 15 minutes.

Meanwhile, prepare the broth by combining the soy sauce, mirin, sake, and dashi in a small pot over low heat. Cover the pot and let it simmer.

To fry the tofu, place enough oil in a small pot to cover the height of the tofu, about 2 inches, and heat to 375°F. While the oil is heating up, place the starch in a shallow bowl and roll the pressed tofu in it, evenly coating each piece on all sides then setting aside.

Once the oil is hot, place one or two tofu blocks at a time into the pot and let cook for about 4 minutes, until lightly browned. Turn the tofu as it's cooking as needed, being gentle so as not to disturb the coating. Take care not to add too much tofu to the pot at once, or the oil's temperature will fluctuate too much and make perfect frying more difficult.

Remove the tofu from oil and let drain briefly on paper towels, then transfer it to serving bowls and pour the warm broth on top. Serve immediately, topped with green onions and daikon.

Alternatively, decorate the tops of one or more tofu blocks with Sai's Edible Ink (see page 100). Garnish with green onions and daikon, and serve broth on the side.

COOK-NIN NOTE: Do you find yourself eating tofu often? A good tofu press is a great investment to ensure the best texture and even cooking for all types of tofu, especially when frying or sautéing!

SAI'S EDIBLE INK

With its salty teriyaki flavor, this ink pairs well with lightly seasoned foods.

LEVEL: GENIN
PREP TIME: 5 MINUTES
COOK TIME: 15 MINUTES
YIELD: ⅓ CUP

½ teaspoon squid ink

¼ cup dashi

¼ cup soy sauce

¼ cup mirin

2 tablespoons sugar

Combine all the ingredients in a small pot and bring to a boil over high heat.

Turn the heat down to low and simmer until it's reduced by at least half and a thick consistency is achieved. Remove from the heat and let cool.

Once cool, transfer to a plastic squeeze bottle to use. Or use it to decorate food using a clean watercolor brush.

INO'S CHERRY TOMATO SALAD

Raised in a flower shop, Ino Yamanaka has an appreciation for delicacy, which may be the reason she prefers cherry tomatoes over larger varieties. This recipe uses soy and vinegar to provide boldness and tang, while supporting the tomato flavor. With her florist's eye, Ino insists on fresh parsley for garnish and color when plating this dish.

LEVEL: GENIN
PREP TIME: 15 MINUTES
YIELD: 4 SERVINGS

½ onion, grated

1 tablespoon rice vinegar

1 tablespoon soy sauce

2 tablespoons sesame oil

1 teaspoon sugar

2 cups cherry tomatoes, halved

Salt and pepper

Chopped parsley for garnish

Combine the onion, rice vinegar, soy sauce, sesame oil, and sugar in a small bowl and set aside for about 15 minutes to let flavors combine.

Right before serving, sprinkle the tomatoes with salt and pepper to taste, then toss in the prepared dressing. Garnish with parsley to serve.

SHINO'S BEETLES IN WILD GRASS SALAD

With a preference for wild greens to fuel both him and his ninja bug friends, Shino Abur-ame is a natural namesake for this delicious dish. The sprinkling of sesame seeds on top is a reminder of Shino's beetles; it's up to you whether to provide a full swarm or just a few stragglers.

LEVEL: GENIN
PREP TIME: 15 MINUTES
YIELD: 4 SERVINGS
SPECIAL EQUIPMENT: SPICE GRINDER OR FOOD PROCESSOR

2 cups loosely packed mixed salad leaves (include Japanese favorites, if possible, like komatsuna, mizuna, or even a little bit of shiso)

FOR THE DRESSING

2 tablespoons toasted sesame seeds, plus more for garnish

1 tablespoon sesame oil

1 tablespoon miso

2 inches fresh ginger, grated

2 tablespoons dashi

1 tablespoon rice vinegar

1 tablespoon soy sauce

1 tablespoon sugar

Pepper

Prepare the leaves by tearing them up into bite-size pieces and placing in a bowl of ice water for a few minutes to crisp up, if needed, then drain and pat dry.

To make the dressing, place the sesame seeds in a spice grinder or food processor and grind until smooth. Combine the sesame oil, miso, ginger, dashi, rice vinegar, soy sauce, sugar, and pepper to taste in a small bowl and stir well to combine. Let the dressing sit in the fridge for at least 15 minutes to let the flavors combine.

Place the salad leaves in individual serving bowls, then dress just before serving, sprinkling additional sesame seeds, as desired, on top.

BROCK LEE GOMA-AE

This sesame-dressed salad is often made with spinach. But take a stalk of broccoli and dip its crown in soy sauce . . . does the slim, green, round-headed, dark-crowned shape remind you of anybody?

LEVEL: GENIN
PREP TIME: 20 MINUTES
COOK TIME: 5 MINUTES
YIELD: 4 SERVINGS
SPECIAL EQUIPMENT: SPICE GRINDER OR FOOD PROCESSOR

3 tablespoons sesame seeds

½ tablespoon sugar

2 tablespoons soy sauce

1 tablespoon dashi

2 cups broccoli florets or broccolini

Place the sesame seeds in a small pot over medium heat and toast until fragrant and lightly browned, stirring occasionally. Let cool, then place in a spice grinder or food processor and grind well.

Place the ground seeds in a small bowl. Add the sugar, soy sauce, and dashi and let sit for 15 minutes until the flavors combine.

Place a small pot full of water over medium heat and bring to a boil. Add the broccoli, then let simmer for about 3 minutes, until the color just starts to turn a more vibrant green. Drain in the sink using a colander, then place under cool running water for a few minutes to prevent further cooking.

Using your hands, squeeze out any remaining water from the broccoli, then place in a bowl and combine with the sesame sauce.

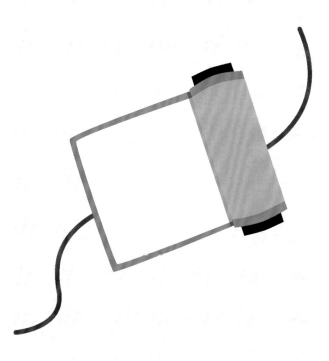

CHAPTER SEVEN: DESSERTS AND SWEETS

As far as we know, there's no Land of Sweets among the shinobi nations, but the Dango Shop in Konohagakure may be the next best thing. It seems to do a brisk business, proving that not even ninja can resist a sweet treat. So don't feel bad if you indulge in these confections. Just be sure to make enough for every ninja on your team.

KONOHAGAKURE ACADEMY
MISSION #7: LET'S MAKE ANKO!

Nothing encapsulates the world of wagashi, or traditional Japanese confectionery, quite like anko. In shinobi terms, it's like a chakra that empowers a wide range of delicious treat recipes. A sweetened red bean paste with a smooth, sweet texture, anko is a versatile ingredient that can be used as a filling, a topping, or a soup, and it can even be served all on its own. Leaving it chunky, called tsubu-an in Japanese, makes a great base for soups and toppings. When using it as a filling, a smoother paste, called koshi-an, can provide a creamier texture. Either way, mastering this recipe is the cook-nin's key to an infinite variety of dessert jutsus!

RED BEAN PASTE: ANKO

LEVEL: GENIN
PREP TIME: 5 MINUTES
COOK TIME: 2 HOURS
YIELD: 8 SERVINGS
SPECIAL EQUIPMENT: FINE-MESH SIEVE

1 cup dried red beans, preferably adzuki beans, but kidney or other red beans will also work

1 cup sugar

Pinch salt

Rinse the beans in a colander to remove any surface dirt. Remove any broken beans, then drain well.

Place the drained beans in a large pot, then add water until there's about 2 inches of water on top. Bring to a boil over medium-high heat, then immediately drain the beans in a colander.

Return the beans to the pot and add the same amount of cold water as used for the first round of cooking. Bring to a boil over medium-high heat, then cover with a tight-fitting lid, turn the heat down to low, and let simmer for about 90 minutes. Check occasionally to make sure the water level is still well above the beans, adding a little more water as needed.

To check for doneness, take a bean out of the pot and press between your fingers. If it mashes easily, it's done. Otherwise, continue to simmer, checking every half hour, until the right consistency is achieved.

Drain the beans, then return them to the pot.

To make tsubu-an, add the sugar and salt. Stir gently until the sugar is dissolved. Use the paste in recipes as is, or allow it to simmer over low heat and evaporate more moisture until the desired consistency is achieved.

To make koshi-an, drain the beans using a fine-mesh sieve, reserving the liquid. Using a silicone spatula or sturdy spoon, scrape the beans through the sieve, collecting the extruded paste into a separate pot. Once the beans have been pressed through, discard the skins that remain in the sieve. Add the sugar and salt to the pot, then add just enough of the reserved liquid to make a thick soup. Stir constantly over low heat until a thick paste is achieved.

continues on page 108

SUBSTITUTION JUTSU: WHITE BEAN PASTE

Red bean paste is popular, but other beans can be used to achieve other pastes, typically with milder flavors. This paste is great as a filling, as well as being the main ingredient for the Shuriken Nerikiri recipe that's coming up (page 123).

LEVEL: GENIN
PREP TIME: 15 MINUTES
COOK TIME: 15 MINUTES
YIELD: 8 SERVINGS
SPECIAL EQUIPMENT: FINE-MESH SIEVE, FOOD PROCESSOR

One 16-ounce can lima or butter beans
1 cup sugar
Pinch salt

Drain the canned beans using a fine-mesh sieve, then rinse under cool water to remove excess starch.

Using a silicone spatula or sturdy spoon, scrape the beans through the sieve, collecting the extruded paste into a separate bowl. Once the beans have been pressed through, the skins will remain in the sieve and you're left with a fine bean paste. Alternatively, drain the beans, reserve their liquid, and transfer the beans to a food processor and process until smooth, adding just enough of the reserved liquid to allow the processor to run. Transfer the bean paste to a small pot and combine with the sugar and salt. Stir constantly over low heat until a thick paste is achieved.

HINATA'S ZENZAI

With pillowy rice cakes floating in a warm, sweet soup, the soft profile of this dessert is a good match for the soft-spoken Hinata. Traditionally enjoyed hot in the winter, it can also be served chilled for a refreshing summer treat.

LEVEL: GENIN
PREP TIME: 10 MINUTES
COOK TIME: 15 MINUTES
YIELD: 4 SERVINGS

½ cup red bean paste

½ cup water

¼ teaspoon salt

4 pieces packaged dried mochi

Preheat the oven on the broiler setting, on high.

Prepare the broth by placing the red bean paste and water in a small saucepan. Bring to a simmer over medium heat, then add the salt. Set aside.

Next, prepare the mochi. Bring a small pot of water to a boil, then add the mochi and cook until they're softened. Drain, then transfer to a greased or parchment-lined baking sheet and place under the broiler until the mochi have puffed and are browned on top, about 10 minutes.

Ladle the broth into individual bowls, then top with a piece of mochi and enjoy!

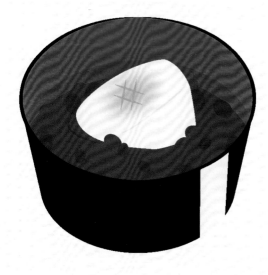

ANKO'S SYRUP-COATED DANGO

Skewered dango are a popular way to enjoy rice cakes; served on a stick, they're highly portable. This recipe is a popular choice at the Dango Shop in Konohagakure . . . especially for the sweets-loving Anko Mitarashi (whose first name is a clue to her sweet tooth).

LEVEL: CHŪNIN
PREP TIME: 15 MINUTES
COOK TIME: 15 MINUTES
YIELD: 6 SERVINGS
SPECIAL EQUIPMENT: BAMBOO SKEWERS

FOR THE SAUCE

⅔ cup water

½ cup sugar

2 tablespoons soy sauce

1 tablespoon cornstarch

FOR THE DANGO

1¾ cup glutinous rice flour

2 tablespoons sugar

¾ cup boiling water

To prepare the sauce, combine the water, sugar, and soy sauce in a saucepan over medium heat. Stir until the sugar dissolves, then turn the heat down to low. Place the cornstarch in a small bowl and mix with 1 tablespoon of water. Stir to combine, then add to the saucepan. Stir again to combine the ingredients, and once the sauce thickens, remove from the heat and set aside.

To make the dango, mix the rice flour and sugar in a small bowl until well blended. Add the water, a few tablespoons at a time, until the dough is squishy but firm.

Dust your work surface with cornstarch, then turn out the dough on top and knead until smooth.

Take a heaping tablespoon of dough at a time and roll into a ball with your hands, then set it aside, dusting your hands as needed to prevent the dough from sticking. Repeat until all the dough has been used up.

Bring a large pot of water to a boil, then drop the dumplings in one at a time, stirring in between to make sure they don't stick to the pot. Cook for about 5 minutes, until they all float to the top, then remove with a slotted spoon and set aside on a plate to cool slightly.

Place a large nonstick skillet or griddle over medium heat and let heat up. In the meantime, take your bamboo skewers and place 3 dumplings on each skewer. Once the griddle is hot, grill the skewered dumplings on both sides until lightly browned, about 3 minutes. Use oil to grease the pan only if the dumplings are sticking.

Once grilled, place on a serving plate and pour the cooled sauce on top.

UZUMAKI CLAN CINNAMON ROLLS

The Uzumaki clan may have scattered after Uzushiogakure was destroyed, but they're honored throughout Hidden Leaf Village, as evidenced by their spiral clan symbol on the backs of the shinobi uniforms. An even better way to celebrate them is with these mouthwatering baked cinnamon rolls. This recipe uses an Asian baking technique called tangzhong to create rolls with a super-soft, irresistibly fluffy texture.

LEVEL: CHŪNIN
PREP TIME: 1 HOUR, PLUS 4 HOURS FOR RESTING DOUGH
COOK TIME: 40 MINUTES
YIELD: 12 SERVINGS
SPECIAL EQUIPMENT: FOOD PROCESSOR

FOR THE TANGZHONG

2 tablespoons water

2 tablespoons whole milk

1 tablespoon all-purpose flour

FOR THE DOUGH

4 tablespoons butter, melted

⅔ cup milk

2 large eggs

3 cups all-purpose flour

1 teaspoon salt

2 teaspoon instant yeast

¼ cup packed light brown sugar

Red food coloring

FOR THE FILLING

3 tablespoons black sesame seeds

¼ cup packed light brown sugar

1 tablespoon ground cinnamon

1 teaspoon salt

2 tablespoons butter, melted

FOR THE CARAMEL GLAZE

2 tablespoons butter

¾ cup packed light brown sugar

3 tablespoons whole milk

¼ teaspoon salt

Start by preparing the tangzhon. Combine the water, milk, and flour in a small saucepan over medium heat. Whisk constantly until the mixture thickens to a smooth, thick paste, about 3 minutes. Remove from the heat.

Turn the tangzhong into a dough by first adding the melted butter to the flour paste and gently whisking until incorporated. Then whisk in the milk until smooth. Add the eggs and whisk until fully incorporated.

continues on page 114

In a separate bowl or stand mixer with a dough hook attached, combine the flour, salt, yeast, and sugar and mix well. Pour the lukewarm flour paste, then stir on a low speed for about 2 minutes, until the mixture comes together to form a dough. Add the food coloring toward the end and keep stirring until fully incorporated.

Depending on the type of food coloring used, this may change the moisture content, so if needed, add just enough milk or flour for the dough to come together but not be too sticky. Cover bowl with plastic wrap and let rest for about 2 hours, until doubled in volume.

Meanwhile, prepare the filling by placing the sesame seeds in a food processor and pulse until seeds are finely ground. Add the brown sugar, cinnamon, and salt and pulse until evenly incorporated. Transfer to a small bowl and set aside.

Prepare the caramel glaze by placing the butter and brown sugar in a small saucepan over medium heat, stirring occasionally until the sugar is dissolved and the mixture is bubbling, about 3 minutes. Add the milk and salt and stir to combine, then set aside.

When the dough is ready, turn out onto a lightly floured surface. Shape into a rough rectangle using your hands, then use a rolling pin to flatten out into a rectangle 16 inches long by 12 inches wide, with the short end toward you. Use a pastry brush to spread the melted butter on top, leaving a 1-inch border along the top edge (farthest away from you). Sprinkle with the filling mixture, spreading it with the brush as needed until the dough is evenly coated.

Starting from the bottom edge nearest you, roll the dough up, creating a tightly rolled cylinder. Pinch the seam closed, then lay on the counter, seam side down.

Use a sharp knife to cut twelve even slices. The easiest way is to cut it in half, then cut each half in half, then cut each of those into three parts. Nestle the twelve rolls with the swirl pattern facing up in a greased baking dish. Cover with plastic wrap and let rise for about 2 hours, until doubled in volume. (Alternatively, if you want to bake your rolls the next day, move them to the refrigerator to rise slowly overnight. Then let them warm up on the counter in the morning while the oven is preheating to finish the rise.)

Preheat the oven to 350°F. Transfer the baking dish to the middle rack and bake until the buns are well puffed, about 30 minutes. Remove from the oven and let rest for 5 minutes before drizzling with the caramel glaze.

SASUKE'S CURSE MARK CASTELLA

Called kasutera in Japanese, this honeyed sponge cake has a long history in Japan as well as in Konoha village. They're traditionally served plain, but the chocolate marble in this variation serves to mimic Sasuke's curse marks—though with a sweeter result.

LEVEL: CHŪNIN
PREP TIME: 30 MINUTES
COOK TIME: 45 MINUTES
YIELD: 1 CAKE, ABOUT 6 SERVINGS

4 large eggs, room temperature

½ cup sugar

4 tablespoons honey, divided

⅛ teaspoon salt

⅔ cup bread flour

1 tablespoon unsweetened cocoa powder

Preheat the oven to 325ºF. Line an 8-by-4-inch loaf pan with parchment paper or grease with oil, then set aside.

In a large bowl, beat the eggs with a hand mixer set on high. Add the sugar, and keep mixing at high speed for about 8 to 10 minutes until stiff peaks form in the batter. It will grow in size dramatically—this foam is what gives the cake lift! Take care not to overbeat it once the peaks are achieved, otherwise it could start to collapse. Turn the speed down to low, then mix in 3 tablespoons of honey and the salt.

Sift the flour into a separate bowl, then add about one-third of the flour to the egg mixture and beat on low speed until combined. Repeat this twice more until all the flour has been combined.

Pour half of the batter into a separate bowl. Add the cocoa powder to the second bowl and stir until combined.

To create the marble effect, first pour some of the plain batter into the prepared baking pan. Top it with some of the chocolate batter, then more of the plain. Repeat this process until you have about ½ cup of each batter left. Draw a knife through the poured batter to create swirls in the cake, then carefully pour the remaining plain batter on top, smoothing it out over the center of the surface. To create the curse marks, pour three circles of the remaining chocolate batter, arranged in a small triangle, in the middle of the cake, then draw the knife through each circle in an outward motion, creating a comma shape with each one.

Bake on the middle rack for 40 minutes, until a skewer inserted into the center comes out clean. If not, continue baking for 5-minute intervals until the correct doneness is achieved.

Flip the cake over on the counter to remove from the pan, then immediately cover with plastic wrap. When cooled, remove the wrap and trim off the sides of the cake, exposing the marbled cake underneath.

Just before serving, mix the remaining 1 tablespoon of honey with 1 tablespoon of water and brush on the top.

TENTEN'S SESAME DUMPLINGS

A popular Chinese dessert called tang yuan, these dumplings are often served for the Lantern Festival in the first month of the new year. Said to be a favorite dessert of Tenten, this food's real-world culture is hinted at by the Chinese-style clothing and hair buns that she wears. While Tenten's favorite filling is sesame, these dumplings can also be filled with red bean paste, or even peanut butter!

LEVEL: CHŪNIN
PREP TIME: 20 MINUTES
COOK TIME: 10 MINUTES
YIELD: 24 DUMPLINGS, OR 8 SERVINGS
SPECIAL EQUIPMENT: SPICE GRINDER OR FOOD PROCESSOR

FOR THE SAUCE

3 cups water

2 inches fresh ginger, sliced

6 tablespoons brown sugar

FOR THE DUMPLINGS

½ cup black sesame seeds

½ cup brown sugar

4 tablespoons butter, melted

1½ cups glutinous rice flour

1 cup boiling water

Red and pink food coloring (optional)

Start the sauce by bringing the water and ginger to a boil in a small pot. Once boiling, turn the heat down to low, cover, and let simmer while working on the other steps.

To make the dumpling filling, first roast the sesame seeds in a nonstick pan over low heat until they've just started to crackle and become fragrant, being careful not to let them roast too long, to prevent burning. (The dark color makes it harder to detect burnt seeds!) Remove and let cool slightly, then place in a spice grinder or food processor and grind until smooth. Mix the sesame seeds, sugar, and butter together until they form a paste, then place in the freezer to firm up until ready to use.

To make the dumpling dough, place the rice flour in a medium bowl and add the hot water. Stir to combine. When the mixture is cool enough to touch, knead the dough with your hands until it comes away from the sides of the bowl and is soft and very slightly sticky; dust with more flour as needed to keep the dough off your hands. It may seem too dry at first, but give it some time to come together before you try adding more water to the dough.

Separate the dough in three portions, then color one portion pink and another red by kneading in a few drops of coloring at a time until the right color is achieved. Leave the remaining portion white. Divide each color into eight equal portions, then cover the dough to keep it from drying out.

To assemble the dumplings, take one piece of dough at a time and roll it in your hands to form a ball, then flatten it out to a disk, making the center a bit thicker than the edges.

Place a spoonful of filling in the center, then gently fold the edges up around it, pinching it together at the top to close. Dust your hands with flour as needed to prevent it from sticking to your fingers. Place the dumpling, seam side down, on a lightly floured surface and continue with the remaining dough.

When all the dumplings have been filled, bring a large pot of water to boil over high heat. While it's warming up, finish the sauce by using a slotted spoon to strain out the ginger from the pot. Add the brown sugar and stir to dissolve.

When the pot of water is boiling, bring the heat down to medium and place one dumpling in at a time, stirring to prevent it from sticking to the pot. (You can cook them all at once, but only cook only as many as you want to eat right away. They don't store well, so place the rest in the freezer until ready to cook.) Cook for a few minutes until the dumplings float to the surface, then use a slotted spoon to ladle them out into individual serving bowls, with one dumpling of each color per serving. Add just enough sauce to cover the dumplings, then serve immediately.

NARUTOMAKI SUGAR COOKIES

Can't get enough ramen in your life? Give these narutomaki-inspired sugar cookies a try. They're just as satisfying as the ramen garnish but extra sweet!

LEVEL: CHŪNIN
PREP TIME: 20 MINUTES, PLUS 1 HOUR TO FREEZE
COOK TIME: 15 MINUTES
YIELD: 12 COOKIES
SPECIAL EQUIPMENT: SUSHI ROLLING MAT

¼ cup butter, softened

¼ cup sugar

1 large egg

½ teaspoon vanilla extract

¾ cup all-purpose flour

¼ teaspoon salt

2 tablespoons flavoring (matcha or cocoa powder) and colored sprinkles

Place the butter and sugar in a large bowl and stir until combined, then whisk in the egg and vanilla. Sift the flour and salt together, then add to the butter-sugar mixture and stir until well combined.

Place a sheet of plastic wrap on your work surface, then spread the mixture evenly on the wrap, making a roughly 9-by-9-inch square. Sprinkle the flavoring over the dough, keeping a 2-inch strip bare on one side.

Positioning the rectangle with the bare strip away from you, start at the near side and gently begin rolling up the dough into a cylinder. Use the plastic to guide the dough, and pull it away from the dough as it's rolled. When the dough is rolled up, wrap it again in the plastic.

To create the crinkled narutomaki shape, wrap the dough log in a sushi rolling mat, pressing firmly once it's fully wrapped to imprint the mat lines in the dough. Unwrap carefully so as to not lose any texture, then place in the freezer to firm up for at least 1 hour.

To bake, preheat the oven to 325°F. Unwrap the chilled dough and cut into ¼-inch slices. Arrange the cookies 1 inch apart on parchment-lined baking sheets, then bake for 11 to 14 minutes, until lightly golden.

Transfer to wire racks to cool.

SUBSTITUTION JUTSU: SHARINGAN COOKIES

You can use the narutomaki cookie recipe to create an endless variation of decorated cookies celebrating the world of *Naruto*. Instead of rolling the dough into a log (step 3 above), roll the chilled dough flat to ¼-inch thickness and cut into circles or other shapes. Bake at 325°F for 11 to 14 minutes, until lightly golden, then transfer to a wire rack to cool.

Decorate your cookies with frosting (see page 121), icing pen, or edible markers to create the Hidden Leaf emblem, clan symbols, Sharingan symbols, or whatever your inner mangaka decides. You can even paint on them using gel food coloring! Add a few drops to a small bowl and water it down until a brushable consistency is achieved, then use a small paintbrush to design your masterpiece! See the facing page for examples.

SHADOW CLONE NINJA-BREAD MEN

Naruto is famous for his ability to summon an entire horde of look-alikes. With this recipe, you can do the same. To shape the cookies, trace a silhouette of one of the cookies shown on the opposite page onto stiff paper, cut out the shape, then use it as a stencil to cut the dough. Or purchase ninja-shaped cookie cutters, which are surprisingly available from bakery supply stores! Maybe we really do live in the shinobi world.

LEVEL: CHŪNIN
PREP TIME: 1 HOUR, PLUS 2 HOURS TO CHILL DOUGH
COOK TIME: 15 MINUTES
YIELD: 12 TO 16 COOKIES

FOR THE COOKIES

3 cups all-purpose flour

2 teaspoons ground ginger

2 teaspoons ground cinnamon

¼ teaspoon ground nutmeg

1 teaspoon baking soda

¼ teaspoon salt

¾ cup butter, softened

¾ cup brown sugar

½ cup molasses

1 large egg

1 teaspoon vanilla extract

FOR THE FROSTING

1 cup powdered sugar

¼ cup milk

Food coloring

To make the cookies, combine the flour, ginger, cinnamon, nutmeg, baking soda, and salt in a large bowl and set aside.

In a separate bowl, beat the butter and brown sugar with an electric mixer until fluffy, then add the molasses, egg, and vanilla and stir to combine. Gradually add the flour mixture, stirring after each addition, and mix until well blended.

Roll the dough up into a ball, wrap in plastic wrap, then refrigerate for at least 2 hours.

When ready to bake, preheat the oven to 350°F. Roll the dough out to ¼-inch thickness on a lightly floured surface, then cut into ninja shapes.

Place the cookies 1 inch apart on parchment-lined baking sheets. Bake for 9 to 12 minutes, until they just start to brown, then remove and transfer to wire racks to cool.

To make the frosting, combine the powdered sugar and milk in a small bowl, then divide into as many bowls as colors are desired. Add food coloring to each bowl, adding a little more sugar if needed to improve thickness, as the coloring may affect consistency. Wait until the cookies are completely cooled before frosting.

SHURIKEN NERIKIRI

While they may not help you win a battle, these shuriken-shaped desserts are just the thing to tackle a sudden sweet craving. Easy to make, no baking required; just shape, let air-dry a few minutes, and eat! (Remember, don't throw them.)

LEVEL: CHŪNIN
PREP TIME: 15 MINUTES
COOK TIME: 15 MINUTES
YIELD: 12 PIECES

1 cup mochiko rice flour

¼ cup sugar

1 tablespoon water

1 cup white bean paste (page 109)

Black food dye (optional)

In a medium pot over medium heat, mix the rice flour, sugar, and water with a wooden spatula.

Add the white bean paste and continue to mix until a tacky, moldable dough forms. Turn off the heat, then transfer the dough to a plate or baking sheet to cool.

Once cool, color the dough with food dye, if desired, by adding in a drop or two at a time and kneading until the color is fully blended.

To shape, take a spoonful at a time, roll into a ball, then flatten into a disk. Use a knife to cut four triangular spaces out of the top, bottom, and both sides, creating the start of a star shape. Use your fingers to further shape the remaining corners into pointed tips. Set aside and repeat the process with the remaining dough.

Let air-dry a few minutes, then serve as is or chilled.

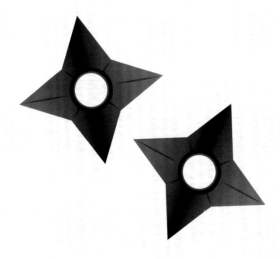

CHAPTER EIGHT: BEVERAGES

If you found yourself wishing to be in the teahouse with Team 7 when they traveled to the Land of Tea, our final batch of recipes can help you re-create that experience. We also have some suggestions to help you unwind after a hard day has sapped your chakra . . . or, conversely, the perfect beverage for summoning a swirl of extra energy.

KONOHAGAKURE ACADEMY
MISSION #8: LET'S MASTER THE ART OF TEA!

After a recent mission to the Land of Tea, some Konoha shinobi returned with a treasure trove of tea-based knowledge. For example, did you know that freshly picked green tea, brewed just right, can actually have a buttery, asparagus taste? Though they're all grown from the same plant, tea leaves can have very different flavors depending on the size of leaf, time of year picked, and even the amount of shade it was grown in. Understanding tea is an excellent way for Academy students to sharpen their observation and sensory skills. And it doesn't hurt to know how to brew a great cup of tea for your sensei.

GREEN TEA TRAINING EXERCISE

LEVEL: GENIN
PREP TIME: 5 MINUTES
COOK TIME: 10 MINUTES
YIELDS: 6 CUPS
SPECIAL EQUIPMENT: KITCHEN THERMOMETER, TEA STRAINER

¼ cup loose-leaf green tea, brand of your choice

For this mission, you're going to do an experiment so you can learn how the flavor of tea is impacted by so few variables, even if it's everyday store-bought tea.

To start, set out twelve small cups that can handle hot beverages, have a tea strainer handy (a fine-mesh cocktail strainer with a handle will work perfectly), and put a kettle of water to boil. Once it's boiling, pour a little water into six of the cups, swirling the water around to warm the sides. Then pour out the water. Next, measure 2 teaspoons of loose-leaf tea into each of the six not-warmed-up cups. (Avoid the bagged stuff for now. Being able to control the amount is a must for tea lovers!)

Use a thermometer to measure the temperature of the water in the kettle, and once it drops to 200°F, pour 6 ounces of water into each of two cups containing the tea leaves. Let one of these batches brew for 1 minute, then strain the tea out of it, into one of the warmed, empty cups. Let the other tea brew for 3 minutes before straining into another empty cup.

Wait until the water temperature reaches 180°F, then repeat the process, again brewing one cup for 1 minute and the other for 3 minutes.

Then, for the last set of cups, repeat the process with water at 160°F. After you finish, you should have six cups brewed according to the table below:

Temperature	1 minute brew	3 minute brew
200 degrees Fahrenheit	Cup 1	Cup 2
180 degrees Fahrenheit	Cup 3	Cup 4
160 degrees Fahrenheit	Cup 5	Cup 6

Now for the fun part: Taste each cup of tea! Which brew is your favorite? Typically, tea becomes bitter at the temperature of cups 1 and 2, so cups 5 and 6 tend to be the sweet spot for ideal brewing.

BREWING MATCHA

Just as there are differences in how tea is grown, there are differences in how it's sold. Most green tea is sold in the form of dried leaves, but for some of the highest-quality leaves, the preparation is taken a step further, and the leaves are ground into a vibrant green powder. The result has a slightly bitter taste, which is why matcha is often paired with small sweet bites in teahouses.

Matcha can be enjoyed in many ways, like mixed into smoothies or added to steamed milk to make a latte. But to prepare a smooth drink with only a little effort, using a traditional bamboo whisk is the way to go! Especially when it comes to getting the perfect frothy texture, the right tool for the job is a must. So grab your whisk and a small bowl, and let's get to brewing!

Generally speaking, there are two types of matcha preparation: usucha, or thin matcha, and koicha, or thick matcha. Thick matcha isn't necessarily thicker—it just uses more of the powder, so a higher-quality matcha should be used to prevent it from tasting bitter.

LEVEL: GENIN
PREP TIME: 5 MINUTES
COOK TIME: 1 MINUTE
YIELD: 1 SERVING
SERVING SPECIAL EQUIPMENT: BAMBOO WHISK, KITCHEN THERMOMETER

1 teaspoon matcha powder

Prewarm a small bowl by pouring hot water into it, swirling it around to warm the sides. Then pour the water out and wipe dry.

Rinse the bamboo whisk with water to prevent the matcha from clinging to it.

For usucha, add about ½ teaspoon of matcha powder to the bowl. For koicha, add 1 teaspoon to the bowl.

Bring the water to 180°F, then add 4 ounces to the cup.

Whisk vigorously with the bamboo whisk until all the lumps are removed and a nice foam develops on top.

HOMEMADE GENMAICHA

In the past, tea was much more expensive, especially when the Shinobi World Wars were disrupting trade. To stretch the tea a little further, many tea lovers added roasted rice to create a subtle nutty flavor. Experiment with different types of rice to find your favorite blend.

LEVEL: GENIN
PREP TIME: 5 MINUTES
COOK TIME: 5 MINUTES
YIELD: 4 SERVINGS

2 tablespoons Japanese rice

2 tablespoons loose-leaf green tea

1 teaspoon matcha powder

Place the rice in a small skillet and toast over low heat until the color starts to darken, about 5 minutes, then remove from the heat and let cool.

Combine the toasted rice with the loose-leaf tea and the matcha. Store in an airtight container until ready to brew. To serve, brew it as you would regular loose-leaf tea.

KURENAI'S SHOCHU MARTINI

This drink uses Kurenai Sarutobi's favorite shochu (distilled from rice and barley) instead of traditional gin or vodka for a martini that's perfect for relaxing after a long day of training the next generation of shinobi. If the day's students included Naruto, she'll make it a double.

LEVEL: GENIN
PREP TIME: 5 MINUTES
YIELD: 1 COCKTAIL

1 cup ice

2 ounces shochu

2 ounces dry vermouth

1 teaspoon yuzu (or lemon) juice

Strip lemon peel

Combine the ice, shochu, vermouth, and yuzu juice in a cocktail shaker and shake well.

Strain and pour into a martini glass.

Take the lemon peel with both hands and twist it over the glass to express some of the oil, then rub the rim of the glass with it to add extra flavor. Garnish with the lemon peel and serve.

KONOHA COSMO

In Konohagakure, it's said that drinking this cocktail is the first step to learning Drunken Fist taijutsu. But if your alcohol tolerance is as low as Rock Lee's, replace the alcohol with a splash more cranberry juice for a refreshing mocktail.

LEVEL: GENIN
PREP TIME: 5 MINUTES
YIELD: 1 COCKTAIL

1 cup ice

2 ounces green tea

1 ounce vodka

½ ounce orange liqueur

1 ounce cranberry juice

1 teaspoon lime juice

Strip lime peel

Pour all the ingredients except the lime peel into a cocktail shaker. Shake vigorously for several seconds, then strain into a cocktail glass.

Take the lime peel with both hands and twist it over the glass to express some of the oil, then rub the rim of the glass with it to add extra flavor. Garnish with the lime peel and serve.

HIDDEN LEAF HIGHBALL

Enjoy served alongside Shuriken Senbei (page 27) or other salty snacks.

LEVEL: GENIN
PREP TIME: 5 MINUTES
YIELD: 1 COCKTAIL

½ cup cubed ice

1.5 ounces Japanese whiskey

4.5 ounces seltzer water

Strip lemon peel

1 sprig fresh tarragon (optional)

Combine the ice, whiskey, and seltzer water in a highball glass and stir.

Take the lemon peel with both hands and twist it over the glass to express some of the oil, then rub the rim of the glass with it to add extra flavor.

To serve, garnish with the lemon peel and, if desired, a tarragon sprig in honor of the forest that hides Konohagakure.

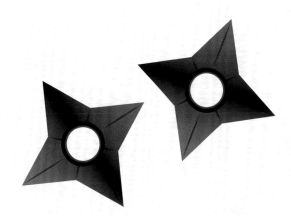

RASPBERRY RASENGAN

Packed with antioxidants and natural sweetness, this smoothie is the perfect thing to power up your day with a swirl of chakra!

LEVEL: GENIN
PREP TIME: 5 MINUTES
YIELD: 1 SMOOTHIE
SPECIAL EQUIPMENT: BLENDER

1 banana, roughly chopped

½ cup vanilla yogurt, divided

1 cup soy milk

⅔ cup frozen raspberries

1 teaspoon matcha powder

1 tablespoon honey

About 1 cup of ice

Place the banana, ¼ cup of yogurt, the soy milk, raspberries, matcha, and honey in a blender, then blend on lowest speed until smooth, about 5 seconds.

Gradually add the ice while continuing to blend on low, adding it until the desired consistency is achieved. Then blend on high for another 15 seconds, until the mixture is velvety smooth.

To serve, pour the smoothie into a tall glass, then add the remaining ¼ cup of yogurt on top and stir a little until a swirl is created.

MEASUREMENT CONVERSIONS

Volume

US	METRIC
⅕ teaspoon (tsp)	1 ml
1 teaspoon (tsp)	5 ml
1 tablespoon (tbsp)	15 ml
1 fluid ounce (fl. oz.)	30 ml
⅕ cup	50 ml
¼ cup	60 ml
⅔ cup	80 ml
3.4 fluid ounces (fl. oz.)	100 ml
½ cup	120 ml
⅔ cup	160 ml
¾ cup	180 ml
1 cup	240 ml
1 pint (2 cups)	480 ml
1 quart (4 cups)	.95 liter

Temperatures

FAHRENHEIT	CELSIUS
200°	93.3°
212°	100°
250°	120°
275°	135°
300°	150°
325°	163°
350°	177°
400°	205°
425°	218°
450°	232°
475°	246°

Weight

US	METRIC
0.5 ounce (oz.)	14 grams (g)
1 ounce (oz.)	28 grams (g)
¼ pound (lb.)	113 grams (g)
⅓ pound (lb.)	151 grams (g)
½ pound (lb.)	227 grams (g)
1 pound (lb.)	454 grams (g)

DIETARY CONSIDERATIONS

V = Vegetarian
GF = Gluten-free

V+ = Vegan
GF* = Gluten Free Using Tamari Soy Sauce

V* = Vegetarian Using Vegetarian Dashi
V+* = Vegan Using Vegetarian Dashi

Chapter One

Classic Dashi	GF	V*	V+*
Leftover Dashi Furikake	GF*	V*	V+*
Kakashi's Eggplant-Mixed Miso Soup	GF	V*	V+*
Konoha Mixed Mushroom Soup	GF*	V+*	
Ninja-Dog Nikuman	GF*		
Tsunade's Healing Zosui	GF*		
Chōji's Chips	V+		
Shuriken Senbei	GF	V	V+

Chapter Two

Japanese Steamed Rice	GF	V	V+
Sasuke's Favorite Onigiri	GF*		
Sand Village Sekihan	GF V V+		
Shadow Clone Jutsu: Hinata's Naruto Onigiri	GF		
Madara-Eye Inarizushi	GF* V* V+*		
Shadow Clone Jutsu: Sanshō's Curry of Life	GF*		
Uzumaki Omurice	GF*		

Chapter Three

Teuchi Udon	V	
Shukaku's One-Tail Tanuki Soba	V*	V+*
Kurama's Nine-Tails Kitsune Udon	V*	V+*
Neji's Herring Soba	GF*	
Might Guy's Overflowing Youth Super-Spicy Curry Udon		
Naruto's Instant Ramen Hacks		
Shadow Clone Justu: Ichiraku Ramen		

Chapter Four

Steamed Fish Cakes: Narutomaki	GF
Fried Fish Cakes: Satsuma-Age	GF
Kakashi's Salt-Broiled Saury	GF*
Sea Monster Tempura	
Eight-Tails Tako Su	GF*
Shikamaru's Simmered Mackerel	GF*
Kisame's Chirashi Sushi	GF*

Chapter Five

Classic Chicken Teriyaki	GF*
Chōji's Yakiniku	GF*
Akimichi Clan Chanko Nabe	
Shadow Clone Jutsu: Boruto's Green Chile Hamburgers	
Shadow Clone Jutsu: Super-Sour Burger	
Sakura's Umeboshi Chicken	GF*
Infinite Tsukuyomi Tsukune	GF*
Akamaru's Favorite Dog Food	GF*

Chapter Six

Quick Pickled Cucumber	GF	V	V+
Yamanaka Flowers' Chrysanthemum Radishes	GF	V*	V+*
Sasuke's Soy-Pickled Tomatoes	GF	V*	V+*
Sai's Artful Agedashi Tofu	GF*	V*	V+*
Sai's Edible Ink	GF*	V*	V+*
Ino's Cherry Tomato Salad	GF*	V	V+
Shino's Beetles in Wild Grass Salad	GF*	V*	V+*
Brock Lee Goma-ae	GF*	V*	V+*

Chapter Seven

Red Bean Paste: Anko	GF	V	V+
Hinata's Zenzai	GF	V	V+
Anko's Syrup-Coated Dango	GF*	V	V+
Uzumaki Clan Cinnamon Rolls	V		
Sasuke's Curse Mark Castella	V		
Tenten's Sesame Dumplings	GF	V	
Narutomaki Sugar Cookies	V		
Shadow Clone Ninja-Bread Men	V		
Shuriken Nerikiri	GF	V	V+

Chapter Eight

Green Tea Training Exercise	GF	V	V+
Brewing Matcha	GF	V	V+
Homemade Genmaicha	GF	V	V+
Kurenai's Shochu Martini	GF	V	V+
Konoha Cosmo	GF	V	V+
Hidden Leaf Highball	GF	V	V+
Raspberry Rasengan	GF	V	

TO MY HUSBAND, EAMON, AND DAUGHTER, GISELLE.

— Danielle Baghernejad

ABOUT THE AUTHOR

A self-proclaimed Japanophile, Danielle Baghernejad has long fostered a love of all things Japanese. After being introduced to the world of anime and manga in college, she was instantly hooked, and ever since has been diving deeper and deeper into various aspects of Japanese culture. Her dream of experiencing the nuances of Japanese cuisine firsthand came true after an appearance on the TV show *Sekai! Nippon Ni Ikitai Hito Ouendan*. Since then, she has worked to make authentic Japanese recipes more available to a Western audience. A foodie by night writing on OtakuFood.com, she spends her spare time in the kitchen with her husband, Eamon, and daughter, Giselle.

TITAN
BOOKS

144 Southwark Street
London SE1 0UP
www.titanbooks.com

Find us on Facebook: www.facebook.com/TitanBooks
Follow us on Twitter: @TitanBooks

Published by Titan Books, London, in 2022.

A CIP catalogue record for this title is available from the British Library.

ISBN: 9781803361413

Photographer: Ted Thomas
Food & Prop Stylist: Elena P. Craig
Assistant Food Stylist: August Craig

Illustrations by Monique Narboneta Zosa

Manufactured in China

10 9 8 7 6 5 4 3 2 1